CW00499183

THE

PAPERBACK

FANATIC

Issue 40

Published September 2018

Issue 40

Published September 2018

Edited by Justin Marriott

Assistant Editor Jim O'Brien

Special thanks to all of this issue's contributors.

Graham Andrews, Tom Tesarek, James Doig and Rob Matthews

Special thanks to Tom Tesarek for additional scans for the Lin Carter article

Correspondence welcome-

thepaperbackfanatic@sky.com

FANATICAL CONTENTS

ARTISTS ASSEMBLE: GUIDIO CREPAX

The artists that work in both comics and paperback illustration just keep on stacking up. In this issue, it's Guidio Crepax who is best known as the creator of the **Valentina** character, a slender female with Louise Brooks hair whose dream-like life is a series of erotic encounters. With a European sophistication and a high-fashion sheen, Crepax's Valentina stories were part De Sade psyhosexuality and part absolute twaddle. For many English-language comics fans, I suspect our first exposure to Crepax and Valentina was in the pages of **Heavy Metal** magazine in the 1980s. The likes of Catalan Communications began to reprint his other material, including adaptations of classic horror stories such as *The Turn of the Screw*, *Frankenstein* and *Dr Jekyll and Mr Hyde*.

When researching for Italian paperbacks I stumbled across some translations of the French men's adventure series **SAS** by Gerard de Villiers which carried illustrations which were obviously by Crepax. They carried the same fetishistic high-fashion meets sexual sadism tone of his comics work. There were many, many on the net, so I suggest you seek them out if you like the examples reproduced on these pages.

GO APE!

In a previous issue Cranston McMillan worked his way through the books tieing-in with the **Planet of the Apes** films and TV series. Soon after I found these 1980s German translations which were published under the Terra imprint, which was part of the Erich Pabel publishing stable which also included weekly horror pulp **Vampir Horror Roman**.

The first three, on this page and top left on the opposite are movie tie-ins.
The Jerry Pournelle is *Escape from Planet of the Apes*.
The John Jakes is *Conquest of Planet of the Apes* (translated as *Uprising of the Apes*).
The David Gerrold is *Battle for the Planet of the Apes*.

There were four George Alec Effingers penned tie-ins to the TV series printed in English language; *Man the Fugitive, Escape to Tomorrow, Journey into Terror* and *Lord of the Apes*.

I assume *Terror Auf Dem Planet Der Affen*, which translates as *Terror on the Planet of the Apes* was originally *Journey into Terror*. The other two translate as *Chase on the Planet of the Apes* and *Ranked on Planet of the Apes*, so your guess is as good as mine!

TERRA
SCIENCE FICTION ROMAN
aus der Perry Rhodan-Redaktion

JOHN JAKES

Aufstand der Affen

Ein Roman aus der weltberühmten Film- und Fernsehserie
PLANET DER AFFEN

TERRA
SCIENCE FICTION ROMAN
aus der Perry Rhodan-Redaktion

GEORGE ALEX EFFINGER

Gefangen auf dem PLANET DER AFFEN

Ein Roman aus der weltbe-
rühmten Film- und
Fernsehserie

TERRA
SCIENCE FICTION ROMAN
aus der Perry Rhodan-Redaktion

GEORGE ALEC EFFINGER

Hetzjagd auf dem PLANET DER AFFEN

Ein Roman aus der
weltberühmten Film-
und Fernsehserie

TERRA
SCIENCE FICTION ROMAN
aus der Perry Rhodan-Redaktion

GEORGE ALEC EFFINGER

Terror auf dem PLANET DER AFFEN

Roman aus der weltberühmten Film- und Fernsehserie

ROBERT BONFILS

Bonfils (1922-2018) was one of the most prolific artists to find employ in the sleaze paperback industry where he worked for many of the earliest imprints until carving out his own niche at the Greenleaf imprints. Distinctive for his bold colours and bodacious blondes with just-got-out-of-bed-hair, Bonfils produced the funniest, most psychedelic and surrealistic adult paperback illustrations. His covers for spy-spoof series **Agent 0008** and **The Man From CAMP** are, as a body, the most collectible and expensive of paperbacks. Bonfils covers also featured on other high-end collectible paperbacks such as *Queen of Blood*, *Orgy of the Dead* and a second edition of Harlan Ellison's (as Paul Merchant) *Sex Gang*.

Bonfils often inserted outrageous sexual symbolism in his paintings, putting furry pants on women to suggest at first glance, that they were nude, or snakes and model light-houses as on *Swap Seducers* (opposite). Even those covers in bad-taste - and there were plenty in the early 70s - were imbued with such an exuberant sense of mischief and a lust for life, that it was difficult to take too much offence. Bonfils' world-view seemed light-years away from the sinister and dark images produced by the troubled Gene Bilbrew, and he never denied his adult work in the manner of a Doug Weaver.

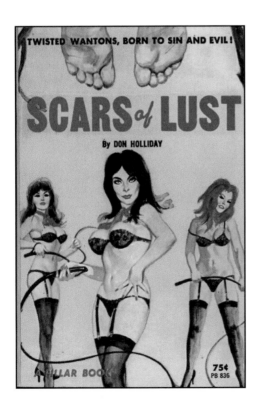

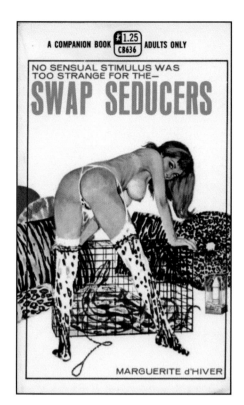

A COMPANION BOOK **1.25** CB636 ADULTS ONLY

NO SENSUAL STIMULUS WAS TOO STRANGE FOR THE—

SWAP SEDUCERS

MARGUERITE d'HIVER

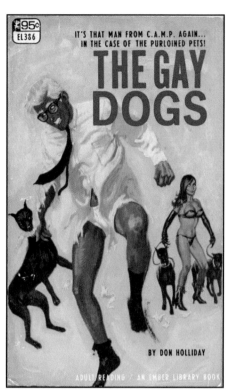

95¢ EL386

IT'S THAT MAN FROM C.A.M.P. AGAIN... IN THE CASE OF THE PURLOINED PETS!

THE GAY DOGS

BY DON HOLLIDAY

ADULT READING / AN EMBER LIBRARY BOOK

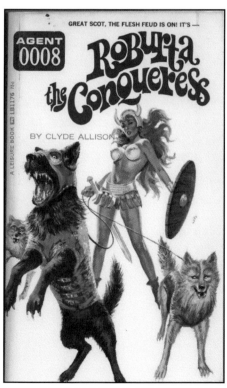

AGENT 0008

GREAT SCOT, THE FLESH FEUD IS ON! IT'S —

Roburta the Conqueress

BY CLYDE ALLISON

A LEISURE BOOK LB1176 75¢

CB545

A COMPANION BOOK | ADULT READING

THAT MAN FROM C. A. M. P. COMES FOR CHRISTMAS!

HOLIDAY GAY

BY DON HOLLIDAY

JUSTIN MARRIOTT reviews the first five books from Richard Laymon, the cult author who bought together horror and crime, but split critical opinion.

BEWARE - RICHARD LAYMON!

Whilst recently discussing a number of horror authors during a social catch-up with a fellow paperback fanatic, the name of author Richard Laymon (1947-2001) came up. 'That's the monster dick guy, right?' laughed my companion. I nodded sagely but realised that I couldn't respond, as I hadn't actually read any Laymon. I had absorbed online comments that his books were downright sleazy in tone and read as if written by a sex-offender-in-recovery, with recurring motifs such as women-in-peril sporting red shorts which revealed their rump, but I hadn't actually read one.

So, never wanting to be short of an opinion, I went about tackling the first five horror novels by the Monster Dick guy. And I can confirm that Richard (or should that be Dick?) Laymon does indeed go into a detailed description of a penis with jaws as sported by a hairy, rapacious beast in his debut novel, *The Cellar*. Talk about starting as you mean to go on....

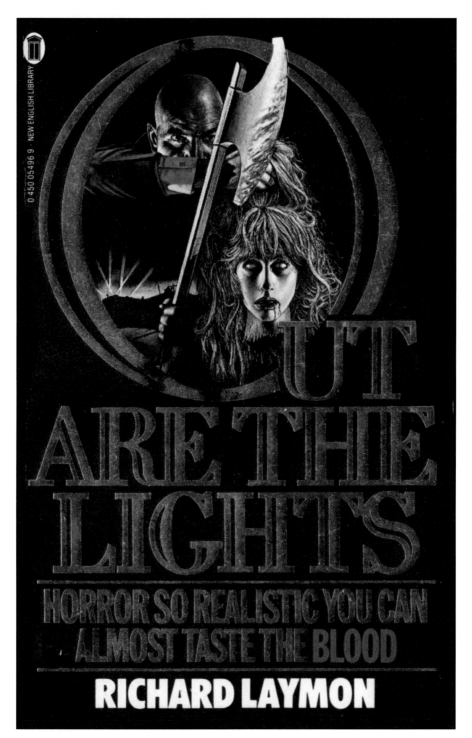

Out Are the Lights
1982, New English Library UK
Art- Uncredited Stuart Bodek

The Cellar (1980) was originally called *Beast House*, but was changed by the US publisher to avoid confusion with the **National Lampoon** film *Animal House*. It's the story of a family of sub-humanoids that dwell in the cellar of a haunted-house attraction. Follow-up *The Woods Are Dark* (1981) was Laymon's survivalist-horror, his version of Wes Craven's notorious *The Hills Have Eyes,* and features a secluded community in a symbiotic relationship with a clan of cannibals. The next two books had strong links to splatter movies: *Out Are the Lights* (1982) paralleled the creations of a snuff-movie maker with that of mainstream horror flicks, while *Night Show* (1984) is set in the world of low-budget horror films, with the female "queen of special effects" stalked by a demented super-fan. *Beware* (1985) features a sex-criminal who has been granted invisibility through an occult ceremony, who then embarks on a cross-country pursuit of his female victim who hides-out in a series of cheap motels.

There is no doubting that Laymon is an 'auteur'. There would be no mistaking his short chapters, dialogue propelled story-telling and sparse descriptions for anyone else's work. In this aspect they reminded me of popular contemporary thrillers written by Dan Brown or Lee Child – easy to pick up and put down.

The books are also set in the Laymonverse (and thinking of them in this way helped me deal with some of the less savoury aspects of his output), which exists only in small-town America, its neon-lit diners which open 24 hours, roach motels with paper-thin walls and flickering signage, and deserted back-

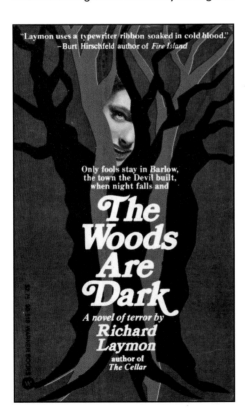

The Woods Are Dark
1981
Warner US

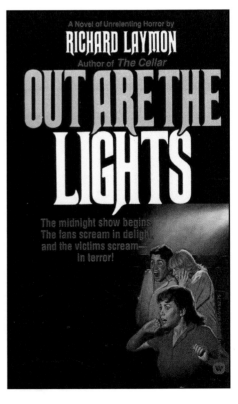

Out Are the Lights
1983
Warner US

roads. And where there doesn't appear to be any police force, whatsoever.

In the Laymonverse, there's no need to gently build the scenario before pulling the protagonists into the action. Within a few pages of *The Cellar*, two strangers have teamed up over coffee to make an off-the-grid visit to the local haunted house in search of horny sub-humanoids. In *The Woods Are Dark*, a pair of travelling buddies stop off at the wrong diner, so as well as tasting some fine pie they are taken captive by the other customers who chain them up to a tree as an offering to the local flesh-eating in-breds. It may not be logical or stand up to scrutiny, but Laymon is not about that, he just wants to pull you into the story as soon as he can. And he is damn effective at doing so.

Everyone gets a rough time in the Laymonverse, but especially women. They are typically victims of abuse: on-the-run from a just-released child-rapist in *The Cellar*, controlled by a scheming boyfriend in *The Night Show*, or fleeing from an invisible rapist in *Beware*.

Rape is a constant threat in the Laymonverse and his descriptions of rape are more realistic than his scenes of consensual sex, which at times are laughable. From a distance, Laymon is as guilty as many other horror writers of the 80s in his portrayal of rape (and I would argue that some were truly misogynistic), which was a key reason for my eschewing horror fiction from that era for some time. Where Laymon delivers a greater punch though, is through the sleazy, leering tone of the writing – as if you are reading the inner thoughts of a paedophile or rapist.

One scene in *The Cellar* that has stayed with me is when the rapist has kidnapped a young girl and Laymon sets up a scene where he nearly gets caught, but it's all told from the viewpoint of the kidnapper, and structured so that the reader should be relieved as he

avoids capture. I found that an especially disturbing sequence and, whether intentional or not, a masterful manipulation of the reader.

Through-out the first five Laymons, I didn't find any examples to support the theory of Laymon's obsession with girls-in-shorts, but nipples showing through t-shirts was something of an ever-present.

Laymon is obviously a fan of the grotesque and Grand Guignol, with his books sharing the tone of the more extreme splatter and slasher movies of the same era. His stories did read like film scripts to me, very much propelled by dialogue and with little in the way of description or insight into his characters' motivations. Laymon's characters don't think, they do and tell the reader what they are doing. This approach did make some of his stories hard to follow, especially at some of his lightning-paced finales, where the twists-and-turns are delivered like axe-blows from a rapist-maniac.

He was unique in his combination of horror and crime, often initially as two separate plots, which conjoin at the book's climax. In an interview, Laymon explained that his early efforts at dark suspense were unsuccessful in being published as they were too sadistic, and he made a conscious choice to switch to horror having read *Salem's Lot*.

Based on low expectations, I had a good time with a couple of these early efforts. For the most part, the Laymons I dived into were unpretentious, drag 'em-out, bad-taste horror books. At times it did feel more voyeuristic and sexually creepy than I was comfortable with, but then when was horror fiction ever meant to make you feel comfortable?

My verdict on the individual titles? *The Cellar* is so uninterested in any conventions of believability and unfiltered by any sense of

Out Are the Lights
1986, New English Library UK
Later editions removed the corpse and featured only the axe-man.

Night Show
1984, New English Library

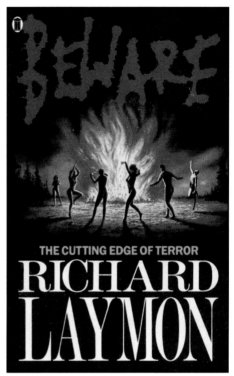

Beware
1990, 2nd edition, New English Library UK
Art- uncredited Steve Crisp

taste, with equal-opportunity rapist monsters (one character returning to face his literal demons at the Beast House refuses to discuss the origin of the clawed-scars on his back) and a downbeat ending, it transcends into a sleaze-horror classic. *Beware* I would recommend with reservations, due to the needlessly detailed rape scenes, but its premise of a psychopath with the power of invisibility and the presence of a kick-ass satanic cult-buster are definite plus points. *The Woods are Dark* is also a bad-taste masterpiece, with the claw hammer-waving matriarch hag of the cannibals giving good head to her victims until a broadsword brings her down to size.

Out Are the Lights and *The Night Show* were both too 'meta' for me in their constant references to **Fangoria** magazine and horror films, plus the behaviour of the female characters (in the Laymonverse they are either scheming nymphomaniacs or easily-manipulated innocents) and cookie-cutter plot made both books turgid reads. Much like a film eschewing plot and tension in favour of gory special effects, these books offer little beyond the splatter.

Laymon's work should be more disturbing than it is, which I attribute to his sparse writing style, which is scalpel-sharp but emotionally detached and lacking depth of characterisation. And for me, horror fiction is all about the emotion and caring about what happens to the protagonists. If you really want your pips squeaked than you should read Charles Birkin for some truly mean-spir-

The Cellar
1980, Warner US
Photo - Neil Slovin

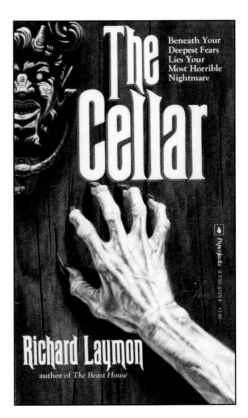

The Cellar
1987, Paperjacks Canada

ited and emotionally devastating horror fiction.

Negative reviews of Laymon (and there are many) can fail to draw the distinction between Laymon as a person and his fiction. His ability to see the world through a pornographic lens when writing and glee in shocking the reader shouldn't be equated with Laymon being a psychopath or a sex-criminal in reality. I did recently read a theory that "slasher movies" are not misogynistic as the finale of a female pursued by a male killer places the viewer in the shoes of the pursued and shares her fear. I don't think this defence applies to Laymon because typically he places the reader in the mind of the killer,

and can encourage you to side with their view.

Slating Laymon, especially on-line, tends to act as blood in the water for his many devoted fans who will not tolerate such attacks on their literary hero. Such devotion should not be seen as a recommendation, as on the whole they do strike me as a myopic bunch, fulsome in their unqualified praise for any of his works.

Laymon was much more successful in the UK than his homeland America, where he blamed ham-fisted editing of his second book, *The Woods Are Dark,* as the reason his career nose-dived. With the success of James Herbert in the early 70s and the sub-

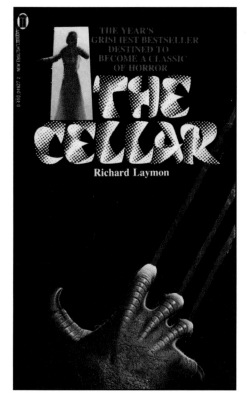

The Cellar
1980, New English Library UK

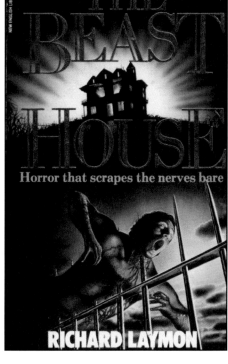

The Beast House
1986, New English Library UK

sequent explosion of 'nasties' from UK publishers, I imagine there was much more of an established market in the UK for a writer like Laymon. He was represented by Bob Tanner, then enjoying success with Shaun *Slugs* Hutson – another author whose early work was very much in the nasty vein.

Watching an interview conducted by Stanley *Dark Dreamers* Wiater – during which Laymon rocks back and forth in his chair like an extra from *Deliverance* on the porch of a swamp-shack – I get the impression that Laymon knew he had a slightly different world-view, one that would be considered weird and sleazy by the standards of normal society.

But quite frankly he didn't give a shit, and even revelled in this. His snicker when discussing the more extreme aspects of his work reminded me of Robert Crumb, the famous underground cartoonist who would respond in that way when called out for his depiction in strip-format of his misogynistic sexual obsessions.

I won't be revisiting the Laymonverse, but that's because his later catalogue increased the amount of crime in his genre-blend which is not to my tastes and there is a rich catalogue of other horror fiction to explore. Ultimately I see Laymon as a harmless kook, who wanted to write crime for Gold Medal and ended up pigeon-holed as a horror author because he couldn't curtail his fascination for the grotesque and the shocking.

LIN CARTER was a regular book reviewer for the idiosyncratic **Castle of Frankenstein** magazine, now remembered as the thinking person's **Famous Monsters of Filmland**. Below is a reprint of his look back at notable genre books for the year of 1965.

LIN CARTER LOOKS AT BOOKS

January

Every year, books of all types jostle for your attention; 1965 was like any other, crowded with new releases and reprints of old favourites. Let's quickly scan (with unjaundiced eye, please) the full year and winnow out a few noteworthy items from the hundreds offered. Leo Margulies produced, in *Worlds of Weird*, a worthy sequel to 1964's collection from the famed **Weird Tales**, again selecting seven good chillers. Best were Clark Ashton Smith's 'Mother of Toads' and Dr Keller's 'The Thing in the Cellar'. Gorgeous Finlay cover and interior black-and-whites. Less inspired was *Shadow Beware* (Belmont), third in the new series of dull Shadow stories that utterly fail to capture the thrilling air of mystery that made the old pulps so charming. A first collection of his Charles-Addamsy cartoons, in Gahan Wilson's *Graveside Manner* (Ace), offered chuckles adroitly served up. A quality paperback of Algernon Blackwood's *Tales of Terror and the Unknown* (Dutton) brought back 11 familiar tales, notably 'The Willows' and 'The Wendigo'. SF writer/anthologist Damon Knight turned to the supernatural with *The Dark Side* (Doubleday), which puts between hardcovers a dozen off-beat tales by Bradbury, HG Wells, Ted Sturgeon, Heinlein, and others – including Avram Davidson's small classic 'Golem', which is (a) science fiction, (b) horror, (c) delightful humour and (d) a refreshingly original lampoon of *Frankenstein*, as well as (e) a thoroughly new twist on the Man-Made-Monster theme. Quite a lot for a short short.

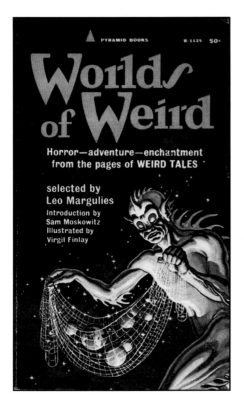

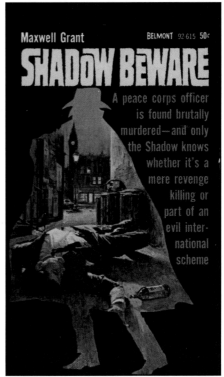

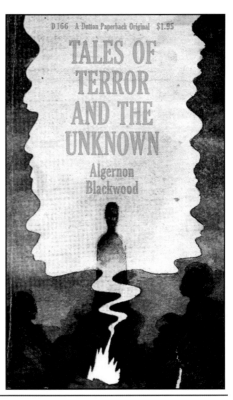

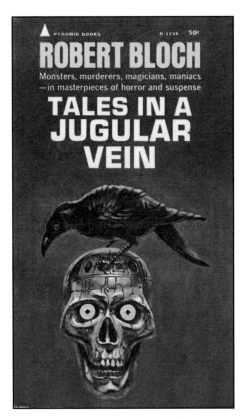

February

Prolific Robert Bloch led off the next month with *Tales in a Jugular Vein* (Pyramid), but the best thing about the book was the stunning Jack Gaughan cover. Better fiction was offered in AE Van Vogt's *Monsters* (Paperback Library), in which the usual ghouls appeared against backdrops of everyday modern life. It gave the familiar monsters a new dimension of realism: you expect them in Transylvanian castles, but it's a jolt to encounter them in laundromats! In the wake of his TV series, Charles Addams held a *Monster Rally* (Pocket Books) a new reprint of his hardcover cartoon-collection, Tarzan returned in *Tarzan and The Madman* (Ballantine), one of the new Burroughs novels, never before in paperback, and good stuff. Some jolly Tibetan-type occult fiction made the scene in Lobsang Rampa's *Cave of the Ancients* (Ballantine) a sequel to his *Third Eye*

of 1964. It comes on like factual autobiography, but don't be fooled.

March

March comes in like a lion with *Tales of the Incredible* (Ballantine), a mouth-watering collection of old EC science-fiction comix - including 'Judgement Day', a pro-integration tale which once upset the Comics Code Authority, and the memorable 'Chewed Out', a humorous extension of a Katy McLean story. (She heartily approved.) Another Addams reprint slithered under the door, *Homebodies* (Pocket). And the Lord of the Jungle made a return appearance in Barton Werper's *Tarzan and the Abominable Snowman* (Gold Star) – 'abominable' is the right word, too. Better fare, for those who prefer their horrors served up as a non-fiction, was Eric Maple's *Dark World of Witches* (Pan). This paperback from Britain, available in a few stores but worth ordering, presented a popular history of Middle Ages witchcraft persecution, tricked out with old woodcuts and engravings. Nice! But best of all – and one of the most valuable books published this year – was *The Serials of Republic* (Screen Facts) in which Alan G Barbour gives a full page of info on each of Republic's 66 serials: complete cast-list, a still and production credits, plus a list of chapter titles! Priceless! How about more of the same on Columbia, Alan?

April

The Doc Savage reprints continued with a gem for monster-fans, Kenneth Robeson's *Brand of the Werewolf* (Bantam), straight from the old Street & Smith pulp (Jan '34 issue) and a whale of a tale. This makes Belmont's uninspired Shadow series look lousy by comparison. Another in the same vein

was the first of a reprint series from the old **Phantom Detective** mag, Robert Wallace's *The Vampire Murders* (Regency). I am less enthusiastic here, simply because Wallace displays pulp writing at its worst, but whoever penned the 'Doc Savage' stories was an excellent adventure-smith, pungent suspenseful, lively. *Ghouls in my Grave* (Berkley) by French author Jean Ray, was the single finest new collection of horrors I read all year. Crisp, economic, dazzlingly different variations of ghoul and vampire themes. Editor Don Wollheim did a Good Thing in reprinting Charles Fort's classic thriller of speculative thought, *Lo!* (Ace). Fort, the great iconoclast and debunker of Scientific Orthodoxy and Sacred-Cowism will be a breath-taking experience for those who have never before sampled his magic. More nonfiction, somewhat less inspired, is Ornell Volta's *The Vampire* (Tandem). This is a popularised treatment of the vampire-myth – and a popular one, too, with editions, in Italy and France, before this British pb transla-

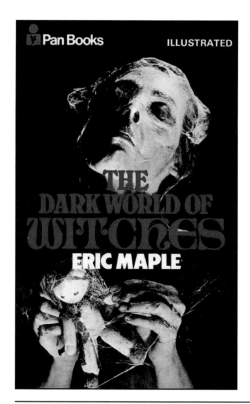

tion emerged from its coffin. Of some interest to you will be Volta's comments on movie vampires (And his illustrations, scenes from films of Lee, Lugosi etc.) and his chit-chat about vampire literature, riddled with errors. (*I Am A Legend* is not a short story, Volta, it's a novel. And you got the title wrong.) Ballantine did the last of Burroughs's Mars books in *John Carter of Mars* (Ballantine) – two un-reprinted mag-yarns from the early 1940s.

May

Dracula is now in the public domain, and the paperbacks are going wild. May saw a nice edition from Airmont at 50c, and others kept coming out all year from Dell etc. Alan Riefe's *Tales of Horror* (Pocket Books) served up 49 short-shorts, all previously unpub-

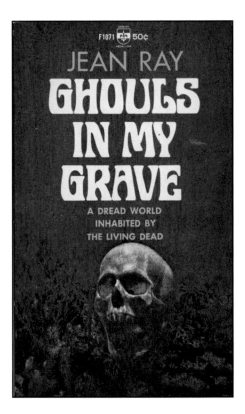

lished and not-bad. A curious format, only 63 pages long, this book is ten inches tall. For monster fans: from Elliott O'Donnell's *Werewolves* (Sic) (Longvue Press) is the first non-fictional study I have seen on lycanthropus sapiens. Sadly for the serious, author O'Donnell's idea of scholarly documentation is: 'a Miss St Denis told me was once staying on a farm here...'. No dates, places, authorities. Still, a hefty, imposing tome. For the monster-movie-fan: Brad Steiger has put together a brilliantly well-chosen selection of 98 stills with commentary in a pictorial history of Hollywood horrors called *Monsters, Maidens and Mayhem* (Merit Books). Get it!

June

Another Doc Savage novel of interest to CoFanaddicts is *The Monsters* (Bantam) a pulp treatment of Dr Cyclops reprinted uncut from the April 1934 issue of the old Street & Smith mag. L Sprague de Camp does a second collection of heroic fantasy on *The*

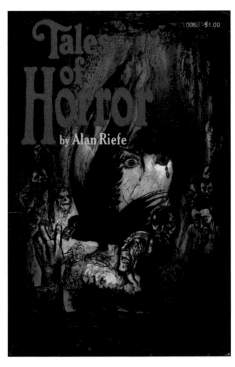

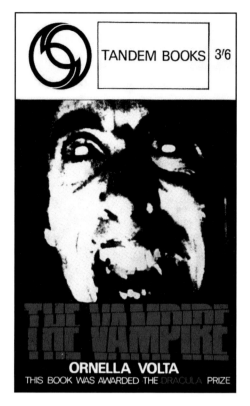

Spell of Seven (Pyramid). It's even better than last year's *Swords and Sorcery*. Seven rare yarns from the old **Weird Tales** days, and elsewhere, by Jack Vance, Lord Dunsany, Fritz Leiber, de Camp himself, others. *Twelve Tales of Suspense and the Supernatural* (Crest) is an off-beat collection of ghostly shorts, arty but satisfying, by Davis *Night of the Hunter* Grubb. The month rounds off with an odd non-fiction *History of the Devil* (Marvin Miller Enterprises) from the daddy of Robinson Crusoe and Molly Flanders, namely Daniel Defoe. What next?!

July

What's next turns out to be Groff Conklin's *5 Unearthly Visions* (Gold Medal); Alfred Hitchcock's *Bar the Doors* (Dell), 13 tales by Bradbury, Wells, Noyes, Bierce, August Derleth, mostly familiar stuff; Rod Serling's *New Stories from the Twilight Zone* (Bantam) all right if you like one-syllable plots – and Philip Van Doren Stern's *Great Tales of Fantasy and Imagination* (Cardinal). Don't be fooled: this is just a retitled reprint (again) of the 1943 Doubleday anthology, *The Moonlight Traveller*. This sunny month was also graced with another ineffable Ray Bradbury collection of creampuff tales; heavy on poetic frosting, skimpy on story-telling meat: *The Machineries of Joy* (Bantam). Monster-lovers should take mote of Tyrannosaurus Rex, a tribute to animators like Willis O'Brien and Ray Harryhausen. Bradbury's OK for those with a mental sweet-tooth and a strong stomach. Give me stuff like *Tarzan and the Castways* (Ballantine), another reprinted, never hard-covered Tarzan novel which rafts the jungle lord to the South Seas and embroils him with a Haggardian passle of lost Mayans, or something. Glorious red-blooded fun, this 24th and last, alas, of all Tarzan novels.

August

A fine bookful of Rudyard Kipling's horror and supernatural stories is *Phantoms and Fanatsies* (Doubleday). White and Hallie Burnett's *Things With Claws* (Ballantine) is back again, but I am increasingly less fond of paperback original collections that get reprinted every few years. Ballantine keeps doing this. What's the matter, can't they get any new stuff? Kenneth Robeson's *Land of Terror* (Bantam) is the eighth of these Doc Savage reprints and has nothing in common with Edgar Rice Burroughs' novel, except the plot... and the title. Jolly, if you like lost islands full of dinosaurs. Happens, I do. More old EC comix in *The Vault of Horror* (Ballantine) – illoed by Jack Davis, Johnny Craig, others; more Bradbury lah-dee-dah in *The Illustrated Man* (Bantam); and yet another anthology is *Owl's Watch* (Crest) from George Brandon Saul, mostly oldies of the yellow-wallpaper monkey's paw degree of anthologised to death familiarity. And a new paperback of The *Wizard of Oz* (Airmont), with an excellent intro by Donald A Wollheim and interior pix by Roy G Krenkel.

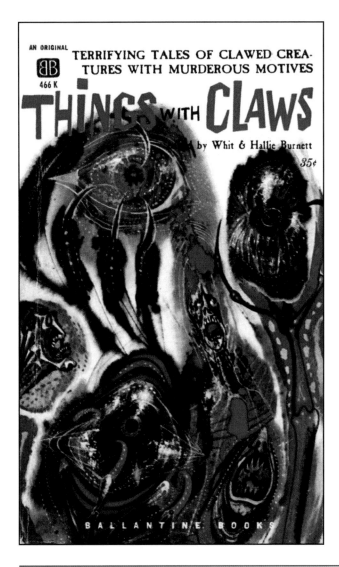

AN ORIGINAL
BB
466 K

TERRIFYING TALES OF CLAWED CREATURES WITH MURDEROUS MOTIVES

THiNGS WITH CLAWS

by Whit & Hallie Burnett

35¢

BALLANTINE BOOKS

September

September saw a paperbacking of HG Wells's durable, charming *First Men in the Moon* (Airmont), poorly timed if they hoped to ride in on the coat-tails of the excellent Nathan Juran movie. Ira Peck produced a collection with the staggeringly clever *A Treasury of Great Ghost Stories* (Popular Library), a yawnsome ten stories, cruelly excavated from their well-earned graves. For those who like their horror straight there was Harold T Wilkins *Strange Mysteries of Time and Space* (Ace), yet one more volume of Marie Celeste Mystery, Lights in the Sky Over Podunk, Was It A Sea-Serpent or Just a Blurred Photo? and I Talked With Granpa Hiram's Brother's Ghost. I'll take the great HP Lovecraft, as in *Dagon and Other Macabre Tales* (Arkham House). These yarns, some familiar, haven't been anthologised into rigor mortis, but they soon will be. A fine book, beautifully printed, sturdily bound. And to make it a banner month, L Sprague de Camp's absolutely brilliant *Spirits, Stars and Spells* (Canaveral Press), an utterly magnificent study of all phases of occultism, Theosophy, the Rosicrucians, spiritualism, alchemy, etc – flawlessly researched, superbly erudite, beautifully written, and as devastatingly keen-edged a hatchet-job as any since Voltaire invented the art of debunking.

October

October means Halloween and monsters, and what name more appropriate than Delos W Lovelace's 1932 novelisation of the Edgar Wallace/Merian C Cooper screenplay of the champ chimp himself – *King Kong* (Bantam) !!!! An excellent novel version that captures much of the boyish enthusiasm and sheer gusto of the best of the Great Big Varmint cycle. Master mystery-writer Edgar Wallace, by the way, here gets a credit at last: he had no scenario-credit in any filming of *King Kong* that I've seen (Now, if the other paperback houses will take their cue from Bantam, there's still Will Garth's novel of *Doctor Cyclops* not yet in paperback, and *The Treatment of Dr Mabuse* and Michael Egremont's gorgeous, mouth-watering *Bride of Frankenstein* – !) CoFanaddicts who enjoyed the Amicus production of *The Skull* will enjoy Robert Bloch's original story in his collection *The Skull of the Marquis de Sade* (Pyramid).

Two new paperback versions of superior Jules Verne novels, both sources for two of the best Verne films, are *The Master of the World* (Airmont) and *Journey to the Center to the Earth* (Penguin). Does Airmont only print books which are in public domain, or do they actually pay an author now and then a little royalty?

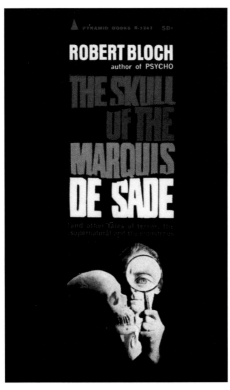

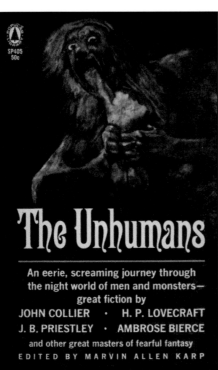

Journey by the way, is a new translation by Robert Baldrick. I am all for this: Verne is only available in crusty old Victorian translations. Get him into colloquial modern English, and more readers will discover what a delightful, witty fictioneer he was! George K Anderson surveys a great medieval legend, including its many incursions into literature, in *The Legend of the Wandering Jew* (Brown Univ Press). The price is absurd, but the book is a fine job. A better-than-average collection of new and old pieces was put together in *A Chamber of Horrors* (Little Brown). Not to mention Pennethorn Hughes' *Witchcraft* (Penguin), a good guided tour through one of the darkest pages of Christian Europe's gory history. And don't let Marvin Karp's *The Unhumans* (Popular Library) get past you: it's good thrills and chills, not science fiction. More Bradbury in *The Autumn People* (Ballantine), reprints from the EC Comic adaptations of 'The Lake', 'Touch and Go' others – with a fine Frazetta cover and a short intro by Bradbury. Irena Karlova – anyone named 'Karlova' could go on to become the Karloff of horror fiction! – did a honey of a vampire novel in *Dreadful Hollow* (Paperback Library), a rare and sought-after hardcover, now in paperback. Don't miss it.

November

In November, a new hardcover series was founded by WW Norton, called 'The Seagull Library of Mystery and Suspense' – quality reprints of rare old classics... famous detective, crime, spy, ghost stories and tales of fantasy, suspense, mystery, adventure and horror. Among the first releases; Arthur Machen's *The Terror* (from 1917, the thriller which dear Daphne DuMaurier must have read before she wrote 'The Birds'); Edgar Wallace's hoary old creepy-crawler, *The Green Archer* (upon which was insecurely based one of the most absurd movie serials of all time). Series editor is Vincent Starrett,

well-known connoisseur of The Good Old Fashioned Stuff. Jules Feiffer turned a nostalgicky, backward gaze in *The Great Comic Book Heroes* (Dial Press), Herbert Van Thal produced yet another of his very excellent horror anthologies *Famous Tales of the Fantastic* (Hill), and one of the earliest of the Original Gothick Romances, Ann Radcliffe's spooky-but-tiresome *Mysteries of Udolpho* (Oxford) was dusted off for another appearance.

December

Santa Claws had a gory goodie in his pack; *Dracul*a is busting out all over, but never more sumptuously than in the beautiful, beautiful Heritage Press deluxe, boxed illustrated edition with a lip-smacking intro by Anthony Boucher.

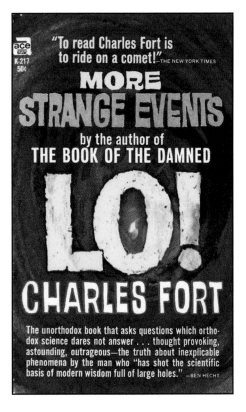

GRAHAM ANDREWS regular column looking at tie-in paperbacks, traces the journey of *Gideon of Scotland Yard* by the phenomenally prolific John Creasey (as J J Marric) from paperback into the film *Gideon's Day* directed by the legendary John Ford.

FIT TO BE TIED: GIDEON'S DAY

Film/TV tie-in books don't always take the form of paperback originals, e.g. *Rio Bravo* and *Dr. Terror's House of Horrors*. Classic and/or bestselling novels have also been turned into 'major' films, with suitably repackaged editions. Random harvest: *Wuthering Heights* and – well – *Random Harvest*. These days, the reprint tie-in tends to be a perfunctory affair. Stills/credits on front and back covers, with little evidence of input from the publisher's design team (if any). But there was a time...

The ten-year period 1955-65 was particularly rich in imaginative tie-in cover artwork. Gold Medal (USA) and Panther (UK) brought out many volumes that transcended the lazy film-poster look. For the purposes of this article, however, I'd like to discuss the British and American promo editions of *Gideon's Day*, by JJ Marric (aka John Creasey).

I can only hint, here, at the fantastic career of John Creasey (17 September 1908 to 9 June 1973): 500+ novels under 20+ pseudonyms, and over 60 million copies of his books have been sold worldwide. He created several long-running series, notably the Toff (58 titles), Inspector West (43 titles), Dr Palfrey (31 titles), and – as Anthony Morton – the Baron (49 titles). Read all about it in *John Creasey – Fact or Fiction? A Candid Commentary in Third Person, With a Bibliography by John Creasey and Robert E. Briney* (Armchair Detective Press, White Bear Lake, Minnesota, 1968: revised edition, 1969).

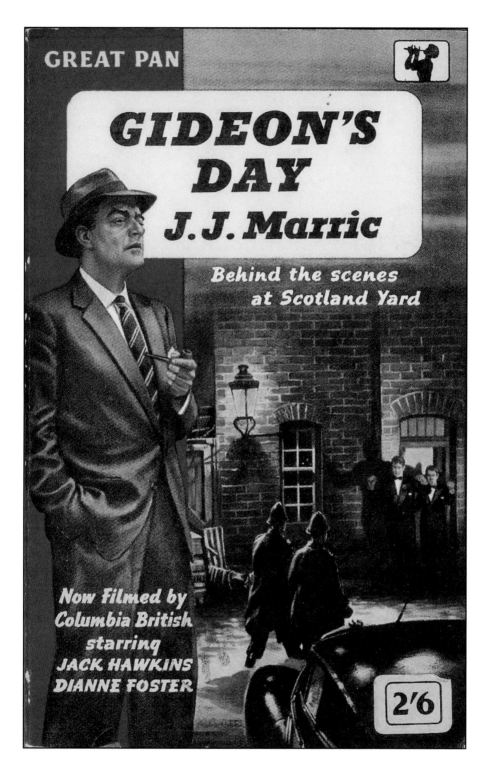

GREAT PAN

GIDEON'S DAY
J. J. Marric

Behind the scenes
at Scotland Yard

Now Filmed by
Columbia British
starring
JACK HAWKINS
DIANNE FOSTER

2'6

Gideon's Day
1955, Pan Books UK

But it was Gideon (21 titles) that gave Creasey his largest measure of critical acclaim. He pioneered the British police procedural novel as we know it today (Wexford, Morse, Banks, etc.), the year before Ed McBain's 87th Precinct did the same for American crime fiction. Julian Symons recognised this achievement in *Bloody Murder* (Faber & Faber, London, and Harper, (as *Mortal Consequences*) New York, 1972. Revised 1985): 'The portrait of Gideon is an attempt to show a fully rounded character, excellent up to a point but marred in the end by excessive hero-worship, and lack of humour. Apart from Gideon the strengths of the books are those of other Creasey work, an apparently inexhaustible flow of ideas and the ability to generate excitement in describing action.' (1974, Penguin edition, p. 210).

Surprisingly enough, Creasey's work didn't hold much appeal for filmmakers. The Honourable Richard Rollison appeared in two mediocre second features: *Salute the Toff* (1951, starring Tony Britton) and *Hammer the Toff* (1952, starring John Bentley). But *Gideon's Day* (1958) was financed by Columbia, a minor-major/major-minor Hollywood studio, and directed by John Ford.

From 1917, John Ford (1 February 1894-31 August 1973) directed some 50 features and umpteen short features. His best work includes: *The Informer* (1935), *Stagecoach* (1939), *The Grapes of Wrath* (1940), *How Green Was My Valley* (1941), *The Quiet Man* (1952), *The Searchers* (1956), and *The Man Who Shot Liberty Valance* (1962). Recommended reading: *John Ford: The Man and his Films* (University of California Press, 1986), by Tag Gallagher.

By the mid-1950s, Ford's career was faltering because of illness and alcoholism. He got laid off from *Mister Roberts* (1955: completed by Mervyn LeRoy) for 'health reasons' – a ruptured gall bladder. But his punching out of the star, Henry Fonda, might also have had something to do with it. The three films he made after *The Searchers* didn't set the cinematic world on fire: *The Wings of Eagles*, *The Rising of the Moon* (both 1957), and *The Last Hurrah* (1958: the best of the bunch, from Edwin O'Connor's feisty political novel).

Ford, however, craved independence and didn't mind the occasional box-office flop. Although commanding over $250,000 per film, he often made 'home movies' for next to nothing, e.g. *The Rising of the Moon*, which got lost in the Celtic twilight. *Gideon's Day* was another Ford near-freebie, but one that could turn a profit-share – however small. The Hitchcock emergency formula: big-name director + reliable actors + best-selling novel bought cheap + minimal work rate = running for cover. The production values belie the low negative cost ($543,000) and Ford did much more than point the camera. Thirty episodes and 50 speaking parts have been crammed into 91 minutes. The cast list reads like a *Who's Who* of British and Irish character actors, headed by the stalwart Jack Hawkins (14 September 1910 to 18 July 1973).

Jack Hawkins made his first movie, *Birds of Prey* (American title: *The Perfect Alibi*) in 1930. Then came Hitchcock's 1932 remake of *The Lodger*, *The Good Companions* (1933), and many others. After Second World War service, he honed his stiff-upper-lippery in *The Fallen Idol* (1948), *No Highway* (1951), and – especially – *The Cruel Sea* (1955). Also, the pukka Egyptian monarch in *Land of the Pharaohs* (1955). Hawkins might have been born to play George Gideon (nicknamed GG). Physically, at any rate: 'In his big way, Gideon was distinguished-looking, with his iron-grey hair, that [hooked] nose, arched lips, a big, square chin. His looks would have been an asset in any profession from the law to politics, and especially in the Church; they occasionally helped to impress a jury, especially when there were several women on it.' (Pan paperback edition, p.7).

The film employs a limited voice-over narration. It opens with Gideon in full, irascible flow. Again, these scenes could have been lifted verbatim from Creasey's original prose: 'The wrath of Gideon was remarkable to see and a majestic thing to hear... Such times did not come often; but as Gideon was a superintendent [later commander] at New Scotland Yard, whenever it did, it made many people uneasy, and set them searching their consciences for evidence of things undone or badly done. All the sins of omission and commission noticed by Gideon but not used in evidence against his subordinates, became vivid in the recollection of the offenders; on any one of these, Gideon might descend.' (*ibid*. p. 5).

This time, the wrath of Gideon is being visited upon a corrupt detective-sergeant named Foster (changed to Kirby for the film version, in which he was played by the smoothie-chops actor Derek Bond): 'I sent for you to tell you that you're a living disgrace to the CID and the Metropolitan Police Force generally. In all my years on the Force I've met some fools and a few knaves and here and there a rat, and you're one of the big rats . . . We make mistakes here at the Yard, and occasionally let a rogue in, but you're the first of your kind I've come across, and I'd like to break your neck.' (*ibid*. p. 10).

Inwardly, however, Gideon was 'worried in case he had been swayed too much by his fury when handling Foster. Ninety-nine times out of a hundred he would have waited to cool off before tackling the man; this time he hadn't been able to. Every now and again he erupted as he had this morning into a rage which perhaps only he knew was virtually uncontrollable.' (*ibid*. p. 17).

In the film version, Gideon is more Dr Jekyll than Mr Hyde. TEB Clarke (7 June 1907 to 11 February 1989), the veteran screenwriter (*Passport to Pimlico*, *The Lavender Hill Mob*, etc.) hews close to plot and sub-plots. But he also adds liberal doses of his own quirky humour: Gideon buys the wrong fish for his

wife (aged haddock instead of fresh salmon), gets a parking ticket (which he won't fix, on general principle), rips his coat, is interrupted at breakfast, lunch, and dinner. When a sergeant snaps to attention, he remarks that the war has been over for years.

Ford set great store by family values – Walton, not Addams. He placed more emphasis upon Gideon's home life than Creasey ever did. As Kate Gideon, Anna Lee displays all the quiet heroism of a US Cavalry wife at Fort Apache. Gideon is beaten to the bathroom by his flighty-but-respectful daughter, Sally (Pru, in the novel). She was played by Anna (daughter of Raymond, sister of Daniel) Massey, making her film debut. Ronnie and Jane Gideon were, in real life, Malcolm and Mavis Ranson.

The nearest thing to a leading lady is Dianne Foster (Joanna Delafield). Other key roles were played by Cyril Cusack (Herbert 'Bertie' Sparrow), Ronald, son of Leslie Howard (Paul Delafield), Laurence Naismith (Arthur Sayer), Jack Watling (Rev Julian Small), and Donal Donnelly (Feeney: Murphy, in the novel. Feeney was Ford's birth surname, though sources vary).

'Gideon knew that he loved London and after a fashion, loved Londoners. It wasn't just sentiment; he belonged to the hard pavements, the smell of petrol and oil, the rumble and the growl of traffic and unending sound of footsteps, as some men belonged to the country . . . The country hadn't the same feel; he felt that it could cheat him, without him knowing it, whereas here in London the odds were always even.' (*ibid*; p. 19).

Ditto the film version. Although Ford doesn't miss the usual touristy spots, he also hints at the Old London Town few Americans know. Tag Gallagher has claimed that: '... *Gideon's Day* is about London, the British and 1957, about the claustrophobia, craziness and complacent despair of modern life ('London

Bridge is falling down…', mocks the theme tune) and it is surely not unintentional when we glimpse a headline about the H-bomb.' (p. 359). For me, the only sour note is when an escaped convict from Up North is caught because some P.C. Plod spots him reading that day's *Manchester Guardian* (a national newspaper, even then).

Gideon's Day was filmed during the spring of 1957, released in March 1958 (UK) and February 1959 (USA). Columbia titled it *Gideon of Scotland Yard*) for the American market: (a) Scotland Yard pushes certain commercial buttons and (b) audiences might have expected yet another Biblical epic. Jack Hawkins as the original Gideon? Hmmm…

Hodder & Stoughton, London, published the novel in 1955, with Harper, New York, following suit that very same year. The Pan (G-109) and Berkley (G-122) tie-in editions

Back cover to the Pan 1958 paperback of *Gideon's Day*.

both came out in mid-1958).

Despite its scarlet backdrop, there is an air of solidity – even stolidity – about the Pan front cover. Artist S R Boldero was a Pan regular, with Eric Ambler's *The Night-Comers* (also 1958) and many other memorable paintings to his credit. 'Behind the scenes at Scotland Yard' reads the blurb. Hawkins/Gideon stands off to stage right, gazing narrow-eyed at some unseen naughtiness. In the wider part of the cover, two unarmed Bobbies are approaching two shifty characters (with their hands obligingly up) outside what might be a gambling den. The back-cover blurb eschews sensationalism, apart from a vulgar exclamation mark: '**One man's day at Scotland Yard!**' And, in case somebody didn't pay close attention to the front cover: 'Now filmed as a COLUMBIA BRITISH PRODUCTION Directed by John Ford.'

Berkley goes to the opposite extreme with *Gideon of Scotland Yard*. Their front cover highlights these basic human psychological drives: violence, greed, and sex. Jack Hawkins hefts a Webley revolver that might have seen action at the Siege of Sidney Street, in 1910. Greed is represented by an attaché case (banknotes? jewellery? letters of transit?) held by clinging brunette Dianne Foster. Big Ben – the clock tower, not Cartwright senior – stands at phallic attention in the minimalist background. I'd like to credit the cover artist, but I can't make out the squiggly signature. Their back-cover blurb is much more robust than its True Brit counterpart, headed by a *Dragnet*-style timetable:

'**CRIME AROUND THE CLOCK**
10.30 a.m. Mail robbery…
12.55 p.m. A rape murder…
2.00 p.m. Store-keeper killed…
6:00 p.m. Jewel robbery…
12.01 a.m. Gunfight with bank robber…'
Phew! I'd hate to be Gideon on a **busy** day
.

Book collectors should have no real difficulty

in finding the Pan edition of *Gideon's* Day. Pans from that period are incredibly robust: thick spines, acid-free paper and durable covers. It's unusual to see their Gideon tie-in edition looking less than Very Good, with Fine copies almost a drug on the market. However, mid-1950s Berkley paperbacks are generally in the opposite condition to their Pan counterparts. *Gideon of Scotland Yard* is no exception, although it does have a certain scarcity value. Moe Wardle's $2.50 price tag, in *The Movie Tie-In Book* (Coralsville, Iowa, 1994), now lies at least five times wide of the mark. But it must also be said that later Berkleys have proven to be made of stronger stuff. My favourite example: *Castle Skull*, by John Dickson Carr (both the April 1960 and August 1964 editions).

The movie adaptation of *Gideon's Day* was a minor financial and critical success in the British home and Commonwealth markets. French *cineastes* took it to their Gallic hearts: 'The lightest, most direct, least fabricated film ever to emerge from one of Her Majesty's studios,' (*Cahiers du Cinema*). And it fared even better with mystery-mad (West) German film fans. In the USA, however, *Gideon of Scotland Yard* was not so much released as half-killed trying to escape. Columbia consigned it to the 'arty' cinemas showing dangerously 'foreign' films that could then be found in places like Greenwich Village – and probably still can.

Gideon of Scotland Yard suffered a $50,000 loss in first-year domestic gross. A self-fulfilling prophecy, if ever there was one. But its popular and critical reputations have grown over the passage of time. Steven H. Scheuer's *Movies on TV and Videocassette* awards it three stars (Good) out of a possible four (Excellent). Leonard Maltin, on the debit side: '*½. Hawkins is likeable but the film is unbelievably dull... Originally released in the US in black and white,' (*Movie & TV Guide*). You pays your money, and you takes your choice. There was no call for a sequel. The vital box-office numbers just didn't add up.

Originally published as GIDEON'S DAY
Now a John Ford Production, GIDEON OF SCOTLAND YARD

CRIME AROUND THE CLOCK

10:30 a.m. Mail robbery . . .
12:55 p.m. A rape murder . . .
2:00 p.m. Store-keeper killed . . .
6:00 p.m. Jewel robbery . . .
12:01 a.m. Gunfight with bank robber . . .

Here is one day in the exciting life of a Scotland Yard Inspector. In the dramatic space of fifteen hours, he matches wits with hoodlums, dope pushers, rapists and murderers. You'll follow him through the twisted side-streets and alleys of London's crime-infested underworld.

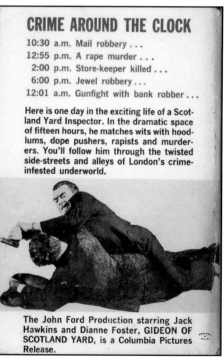

The John Ford Production starring Jack Hawkins and Dianne Foster, GIDEON OF SCOTLAND YARD, is a Columbia Pictures Release.

Front and back cover of the Berkley movie tie-in.

Jack Hawkins went on to consolidate his international stardom with *Ben-Hur* (1959), *Lawrence of Arabia* (1962) and *Zulu* (1963). He headed up *The Four Just Men* (1959), a British TV series loosely based on the Edgar Wallace books, which co-starred Richard Conte, Dan Dailey and Vittorio de Sica. In 1966, however, throat cancer led to the removal of his vocal cords. Subsequent film roles (*Shalako, Young Winston*, etc.) were dubbed for him by either Charles Gray or Robert Rietty. Hawkins finished the ironically entitled *Anything for a Quiet Life* (Elm Tree Books/Hamish Hamilton, London, 1973), just weeks before his death. He recounted some fond anecdotes about John Ford and *Gideon's Day*.

The Gideon books might seem to be tame stuff today. But they can still evoke those simpler years of pure Manichean struggle between capital-lettered Good and Evil. **The Sunday Times** was in no apparent ethical dilemma with *Gideon's Month* (1958): 'Authentic, well told and exciting.' *Gideon's River* (1968) – Old Father Thames – is one of the best late entries, very reminiscent of Edgar Wallace. Creasey/Marric then served a Wimbledon ace in *Gideon's Sport* (1970).

Creasey adapted *Gideon's Week* (1956) for the stage, as *Gideon's Fear* (produced in Salisbury, 1960: published by Evans, London, 1967). Pyramid used the title *Seven Days to Death* for their 1958 paperback edition of *Gideon's Week*. He also wrote several Gideon short stories, including 'Gideon and the Pigeon' (**Ellery Queen's Mystery Magazine**, February 1971). After Creasey's death, William Vivian Butler (1927 to 1987) wrote two further novels: *Gideon's Force* (1978) and *Gideon's Law* (1981).

A *Gideon's Way* TV series (26 x 50 m black-and-white episodes) appeared in 1965-66, made at Elstree Studios by International Television Corporation – ITC, for short. American viewers knew it as *Gideon, CID*. Jack Hawkins being unavailable at that time, Gideon was played by the tough-but-cuddly English actor John Gregson (1919 -75). His filmography includes *Whisky Galore!* (1949), *Genevieve* (1953), and *The Night of the Generals* (1967). His young assistant, Detective Chief Inspector David Keen, was played by the French actor, Alexander Davion (1929 –). A baker's dozen of the episodes were based on 'themes' from the novels. Three of them alone came from *Gideon's Risk*: 'The Big Fix'; 'To Catch a Tiger' and 'The Reluctant Witness'.

Robert Sellers had these kind things to say about *Gideon's Way*, in his seminal study, *Cult TV: The Golden Age of ITC*: 'Shooting on 35mm film, rather than videotape, gave the show much higher production values than other contemporary cop shows, like *Z Cars* and *Dixon of Dock Green*. *Gideon's Way* possibly inspired the police dramas of the future, as it was the first British cop series to escape the confines of a studio and get out onto the gritty streets themselves, filming around London's East End.' (p. 269). The series had a stellar list of stars-before-they-became-famous, including John Hurt, Donald Sutherland, Rosemary Leach, Ray McAnally, Derren Nesbitt and Jean Marsh.

Hodder — Hodder & Stoughton's paperback imprint — brought out some tasteful tie-in editions, with a 'passport' photograph of John Gregson on each front cover.

ITC also produced a one-year — 1966 — series of **The Baron** (30 x 50 min colour episodes). It starred American actor Steve Forrest (1925 - 2013), who failed to emulate the cinematic fame of his older brother, Dana Andrews. The Creasey character was a reformed jewel thief who became an antique dealer and erstwhile detective. Sellers, again: '**[The Saint]** producers ditched the original stories, feeling they were a little out of date for swinging sixties audiences, and turned [Mannering] into a bored Texas rancher living in London as an antiques dealer, while doing a bit of secret agenting on the side. Sort of Lovejoy meets James Bond.' (*ibid.* p. 270).

The New York Times and the London **Sunday Times** ably summed up Gideon in general, and the original *Gideon's Day* in particular: (a) 'The finest of all Scotland Yard series'; (b) 'A single day's work in the life of a Detective-Superintendent at Scotland Yard: factual and unpretentious, this obviously knowledgeable account holds the reader more securely than any stereotyped thriller.' They might just as well have been writing about John Ford's too-long neglected film version — ditto the TV series.

But the perfect last line comes from Creasey/Marric's original novel: 'The hell of it was that this was just another day.'

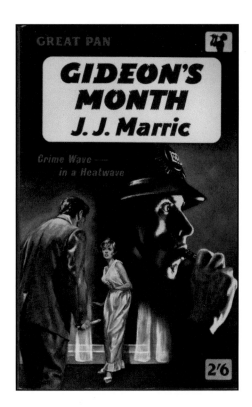

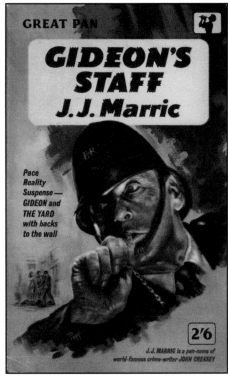

TOM TESAREK takes in a classic of the horror genre in the from of Fritz Leiber's *Conjure Wife* looking at its many paperback editions and film versions.

BEHIND EVERY GREAT MAN THERE'S A WOMAN

When I was young, if I found an author that I liked I tended to become obsessed with them, something that I suspect a lot of readers of Paperback Fanatic can relate to. One author who was the subject of my obsession was Fritz Leiber, Jr. I loved his stories of Fafhrd and the Gray Mouser as well as his science fiction, like the Hugo winners *The Wanderer* and *The Big Time*.

That's why I immediately bought *Conjure Wife* when I found a used copy. It had a Jeff Jones cover like his Fafhrd and Gray Mouser books, but it appeared to be a typical Gothic, with a woman fleeing from a castle with one light in a window. I didn't buy Gothics, but I did buy Fritz Leiber, so I had to get it. And I am glad that I did.

The story begins with Norman Saylor, a Professor of Sociology at Hempnell College, deciding to do something 'a shade out of character, perhaps even a little childish and reprehensible, so that he could be amusedly ashamed afterwards.' He decides to look through his wife Tansy's dressing room, but he is not prepared for what he finds.

First he finds labeled vials with dirt in them that are from various local graveyards. He then finds envelopes with hair and fingernail clippings from people that they know. In the last drawer he finds lodestones, silver coins, herbs and numerous other items, all of which he recognizes from his studies as ingredients for magical spells and protective wards.

AWARD BOOKS AN1143 95¢

CONJURE WIFE

FRITZ LEIBER

DARK SHADOWS
OF EVIL TRAPPED
HER IN A WEB OF
WITCHCRAFT—
A MODERN CLASSIC OF
TERROR AND SUSPENSE

FIRST
PRIZE
for outstanding
achievement in the
field of literature
8th Annual
Mrs. Ann Radcliffe
Award

Conjure Wife
1968, Awards Books US
Art - Katherine Jeffrey Jones

Norman confronts Tansy when she returns home and has her admit that she has been casting spells to help his career and protect them from harm. He convinces her that this is a delusion that she must fight and that the first step in doing so is to dispose of all of the items that she has stashed around the house. She reluctantly agrees to do so and that's when things start to go downhill for Norman and Tansy.

First a student who was getting a failing grade starts to cause problems. A female student accuses Norman of sexual improprieties after her advances are rejected. A question of plagiarism is raised about his work. Finally, after being the frontrunner for the chairmanship of the Sociology Department, he loses it to another professor. Problems just keep mounting.

Without Norman realizing it, Tansy had been advancing his career and protecting them from a coven of three witches, all wives of other university professors.

Leiber slowly builds tension as Norman – and the reader – are unsure if these unfortunate events and setbacks are just coincidence or bad luck, or if there are magical forces at work. But as the story progresses, it becomes harder for Norman to rationalize away some of the events that are happening.

Without giving too much away, more than Norman's career is in danger – their sanity and lives are at stake. As Damon Knight writes on one of the cover blurbs, (when reaching) 'the shocker at the end of chapter 14, I am not ashamed to say that I jumped an inch out of my seat.'

Leiber perfectly grounds the fantastic elements of the story with the appealing relationship between Norman and Tansy and the realistic college setting. Leiber taught at Occidental College while he was writing this and had a background in theater, so much of the infighting and prudishness of a small college appears to have come from personal experience. At one point Norman is confronted by Thompson, the Public Relations

Internal illustrations by Frank Kramer for Conjure Wife from the pages of Unknown Worlds April 1943.

Manager for the College, and is asked about a story that Thompson had heard about a party that Norman and Tansy attended with some theatrical people. 'There was something about an impromptu act staged in a nightclub, and an academic gown, and an…er…strip-tease dancer', to which Norman replies that it is substantially true. I wonder if Leiber was questioned about parties that he had gone to with his theatrical friends.

It is also nice to see Norman give credit to Tansy for some of his success, even if he doesn't acknowledge the magical aspects of her help. In the 1940s Tansy's options were limited, and helping to advance Norman's career was essentially her job. It is clear that they make a good team and truly care for each other. In so many of the stories from this time the women are cyphers, but Tansy is an interesting and appealing character.

I also enjoyed the idea that all women are witches, but men are too oblivious to notice. Unlike many later suburban horror stories, this isn't a small group hidden from the world, but half the world keeping a secret from the other half. In fact, at one point Norman enlists the aid of one his Professor friends who is the husband of one of the three witches. He is more than happy to help, never realizing that what he is doing is helping to thwart his wife's plan.

Conjure Wife was originally published in the April 1943 issue of *Unknown Worlds*. It was Leiber's first longer work, followed closely by *Gather, Darkness*, serialized in **Astounding** starting in May 1943.

Unknown Worlds, previously just **Unknown** was Street & Smith's fantasy/horror pulp. Edited by John Campbell Jr., it shied away from traditional horror stories in favour of urban fantasy and horror, or fantasy with elements of humor. Campbell started the magazine after reading Eric Frank Russell's *Sinister Barrier*. He wanted to publish it but

didn't think if fit in to **Astounding**. With the mix of witchcraft and a modern setting, *Conjure Wife* was exactly the type of story that he wanted.

Unfortunately, by 1943 **Unknown Worlds** had eliminated illustrated covers as a cost cutting measure, instead going with text, so we were denied a cover painting for the story. Also, **Unknown World's** premier artist, Edd Cartier, does not appear in this issue, so we have to make due with illustrations by Frank Kramer, which overall are quite good.

As is often the case, the version that appears in **Unknown Worlds** is different from the published novel. Even when not changing events, Leiber rewrote large portions for the book. However the biggest change is in the ending. In the novel, even at the end Norman is not certain of the existence of witchcraft, while in the **Unknown** version he is a believer. I prefer the **Unknown** ending, as after what they have been through, Norman has to be in a state of denial to dispute the existence of witchcraft.

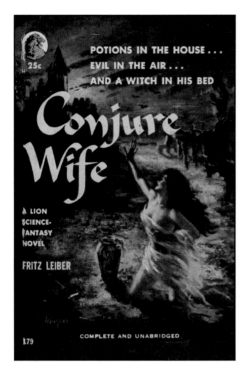

Conjure Wife
Lion Books US, 1953
Art-Robert Maguire

issues of **The Haunt of Horror**, Marvel Comics' horror digest. These printed the text with some illustrations. The first issue has a Gray Morrow cover with uncredited illustrations, the first of which looks to me like Gil Kane, with the others definitely drawn by Gene Colan. The second issue has illustrations by Walt Simonson, a favourite of mine.

The novel has been filmed numerous times. The first, as *Weird Woman* in 1944, starred Lon Chaney Jr. and Anne Gwynne is the only version that I have seen. While it has been years since I have seen it, I remember being very disappointed in it. In this version, Norman's wife is from the South Sea Islands, so

Burn Witch, Burn
Berkley US, 1962

The novel was first published in hardcover in 1952 by Twayne Publishers as *Witches Three*, a volume which also included James Blish's *There Shall Be No Darkness* and Fletcher Pratt's *The Blue Star*. Twayne then published the stand-alone novel the following year.

1953 also saw the first paperback version, published by Lion Books with a beautiful Robert Maguire cover. This was followed in 1962 with a movie-tie in version published by Berkley Medallion. For some unknown reason the film was titled *Burn Witch, Burn* after the A. Merritt novel. In 1968, the previously mentioned Award Books version with the Jeff Jones cover was published, followed in 1970 by the UK publication by Penguin.

One of the stranger publications in which the story saw print was in the first two (and only)

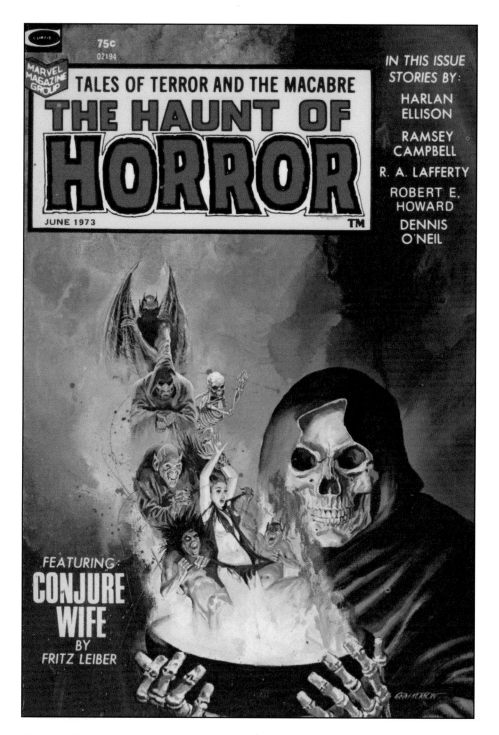

The Haunt of Horror issue 1
1973, Marvel Comics
Art- Gray Morrow

CHAPTER I

NORMAN SAYLOR was not the sort of man to go prying into his wife's dressing room. That was partly the reason why he did it. He was sure that nothing could touch the security of the relationship between him and Tansy.

He knew, of course, what had happened to Bluebeard's inquisitive wife. In fact, at one time he had gone rather deeply into the psychoanalytic undertones of that strange tale of dangling ladies. But it never occurred to him that any comparable surprise might await a husband, and a modern husband at that. A half-dozen handsome beaux hanging on hooks behind that door which gleamed so creamily? The idea would have given him a chuckle in spite of his scholarly delvings into feminine psychology and those brilliant studies in the parallelisms of primitive superstition and modern neurosis that had already won him a certain professional fame.

He didn't look like a distinguished ethnologist—he was rather too young for one thing—and he certainly didn't look like a professor of sociology at Hempnell College. He quite lacked the pursed lips, frightened eyes, and tyrannical jaw of the typical faculty member of that

CONJURE WIFE   5

CONJURE WIFE

FRITZ LEIBER

Conclusion

Illustrated by Walt Simonson

Copyright © 1953
by Twayne Publishers.

NORMAN SAYLOR *is not the sort of man to go prying into his wife's dressing room. That's partly the reason why he did it. He's sure that nothing can touch the security of the relationship between him and his wife,* TANSY.

To his surprise, Norman discovers that his wife possesses all the accouterments of a modern day witch: *graveyard dirt, bits of iron, envelopes filled with snips of hair, and little bags of dried leaves and powdered* vegetable matters—all the *paraphenalia of a conjure wife. As a sociology professor at* HEMPNELL COLLEGE, *Norman has made numerous studies of witchcraft and*

47

Conjure Wife
1969, Penguin UK
Art - Franco Grignani

Conjure Wife
1977, Ace US
Die-cut front cover, full art from frontispiece

it isn't considered surprising that she would be superstitious. While the film initially makes it seem that supernatural forces are in play, it all ends up with a rational explanation, which totally undermines the story. The film is a tremendous missed opportunity, as the story lends itself to a low budget version.

It was next filmed for the television show *Moment of Fear* in 1960 with Larry Blyden and Janice Rule.

This was followed in 1962 by the previously mentioned *Burn Witch Burn*, known in the UK as *The Night of the Eagle* and starring Peter Wyngarde and Janet Blair from a screenplay by Richard Matheson and Charles Beaumont. With that amount of talent this should be a quality production and the re-

views that I have read make me eager to see it.

Finally a version called *Witches' Brew*, aka *Which Witch is Which?*, came out in 1980 starring Teri Garr and Richard Benjamin. This appears to be a comedic version that doesn't credit the source material. Given the reviews it is probably just as well.

Given that Fritz Leiber won Hugo, Nebula and World Fantasy awards, was named a Gandalf Grand Master of Fantasy and an SFWA Grand Master, won a Bram Stoker Award for Lifetime Achievement along with numerous other awards and commendations, there are many of his works for you to discover, but *Conjure Wife* is a great way to start.

ROB MATTHEWS delivers a fine piece of paperback scholarship with a comprehensive study of the **Segretissimo** ("Top Secret") series which provided Italian reprints of a string of espionage thrillers.

THE TOP SECRET SERIES

From a modest beginning back in 1907, Gruppo Mondadori is now Italy's leading publishing house, with a market share of just over 11%, while its many imprints cover all sectors of the market. Formed in Ostiglia by Arnoldo Mondadori, the company began modestly by printing the magazine *Luce*, not publishing its first book until 1912 – *Aia Madama* by Tomaso Monicelli, the first in a series of books aimed at children called 'La Lampada'.

After the First World War, during which time the company published magazines for the troops on the front lines, Arnoldo took the brave decision to relocate his company to Milan in 1919. The acquisition of the literary rights of some of Italy's greatest writers in 1926 gave the company status as a national publisher of cultural importance, and this reputation was enhanced by the launching, in 1929, of **I Libri Gialli**, a series dedicated to detective and mystery stories, the very first being a translation of SS Van Dine's *The Benson Murder Case*. **I Libri Gialli** ran for a total of 266 volumes up until 1941, before the post-war re-launch in 1946 saw the series become **Il Giallo Mondadori**, the title it has kept ever since. So influential has the series been that the word 'giallo' has become internationally synonymous with the thriller/horror genre within Italian film as well as literature – 'giallo' translating as yellow, in reference to the background colour of the book covers.

Gruppo Mondadori introduced another imprint in late 1960 – **Segretissimo** – which translates as 'Top Secret', concentrating more on espionage-oriented thrillers. An initial test of the market saw the publication of twelve translations of the OSS 117 books by French writer Jean Bruce. Bruce, real name Jean Brochet, created Hubert Bonisseur de la Bath aka OSS 117 in 1949, predating Ian Fleming's James Bond by four years. By the time of his death in 1963, he'd chronicled at least 88 of OSS 117's assignments (online sources vary as to the exact number – it could be as many as 91). The series then continued under the pen of Bruce's widow, Josette, for a further 143 assignments, then by his two children, François and Martine for a final 24. The first **Segretissimo**, cover dated October 1960, was *Russia missione A* a translation of 1954's *OSS 117 Top Secret*. The first twelve volumes all featured cover art by Hungarian artist Ferenc Pintér, as well as the

1st volume of the 2nd series, which also happened to be by Jean Bruce – *Le mani nel sacco*, a translation of 1958's *Gâchis à Karachi*.

Cover duties were then taken over by Carlo Jacono, who provided every cover for the next twenty-nine years. Jacono, born in 1929, studied art in Milan and at Brera Academy before producing an amazingly prolific body of work for Arnoldo Mondadori from 1950 onwards. He painted every cover of **Il Giallo Mondadori** from 1950 until 1986, every cover of **Segretissimo** from 1961 until 1990, the first 100 issues of the science fiction series **Urania** and many more – over 3,000 pieces of artwork all told. For **Segretissimo** his covers consisted of a circular piece of artwork on a black surround, usually with a female form in the foreground with a depiction of an action sequence behind.

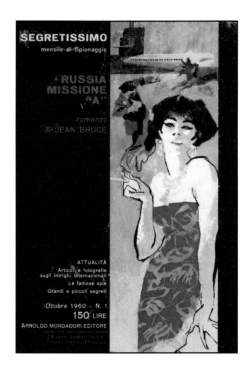

Russia Missione "A"
Jean Bruce
Art by Ferenc Pintér

Egitto Missione "B"
Jean Bruce
Art by Ferenc Pintér

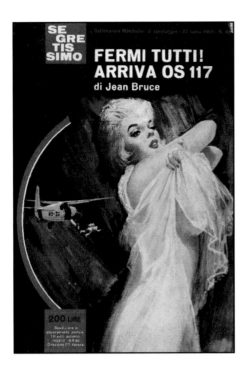

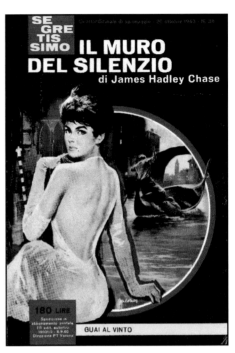

Jean Bruce – Fermi tutti! Arriva OS 117
(OSS 117 joue le jeu – 1950)
Art - Carlo Jacono

James Hadley Chase – Il muro del silenzio
(Mission to Venice – 1954)
Art - Carlo Jacono

Jacono's first cover was for *Il nostro agente a Rio*, a translation of Jean Bruce's *Noël pour un espion*, while his second was for the first non-Bruce entry in the series: *Guerra di ombre*, a translation of the British author Raymond Marshall's *Why Pick on Me?* First published in 1951, the novel detailed how Mark Corridon is coerced back into British Intelligence, after the murder of a friend, to infiltrate an organisation destabilising post-war Britain. Marshall was a pseudonym of Rene Lodge Brabazon Raymond, but Raymond is better known by another of his pseudonyms – James Hadley Chase. Chase achieved instant success, and much notoriety, with his 1939 debut *No Orchids for Miss Blandish*, but his work is best remembered today, perhaps rather unkindly, for a seeming lack of authenticity in the American settings – like Stephen D Frances (Hank Janson) Chase hadn't actually been to the States before setting his books there, his only familiarity coming from American cinema and writers such as Cain and Chandler. Mark Corridon had appeared in one previous novel, *Mallory*, which didn't appear as a **Segretissimo** until 1965, while two other JHC characters, Don Micklem and Mark Girland, also later appeared.

The first American novel to be translated (for volume 5 in February 1962) was Wade Miller's *Sinner Take All* as *L'ora del sicario*. Wade Miller was actually the main pseudonym used by the San Diego-based writing team of Robert Wade and Bill Miller, who had achieved success in the late 40s with their series of novels featuring private detective Max Thursday, before making the leap into original paperbacks when Gold Medal launched in 1950. First published by Gold Medal in 1960, *Sinner Take All* details the assassination plot of a Latin-American political figure in Tijuana, Mexico, and was the

Bryan Edgar Wallace – Operazione: Sterminio
(The Device – 1962)
Art - Carlo Jacono

Edward S. Aarons – Sam Durell a Doppio Regime
(Assignment: The Girl in the Gondola – 1963)
Art - Carlo Jacono

only Miller novel published as a **Segretissimo** although another pseudonym of theirs, Whit Masterson, had several featured in the 1970s, starting with *Spia d'infiltrazione* in 1973.

Volume 7 was the second translation of a British writer, Brian Edgar Wallace, the son of Edgar Wallace, one of the biggest names in early 20th Century British publishing. The younger Wallace, though he wasn't as prolific or as successful as his father, had both of his novels starring British agent Bill Tern translated into **Segretissimo**, the first of them being his *Death Packs a Suitcase* as *La Morte fa la valigia* in April 1962. Randall Masteller of spyguysandgals.com described the novels as '...both entitled to some acclaim for their innovation.'

The first long-running American series to be translated made its first two appearances

with volumes 10 and 14 in July and November 1962 respectively. Although Edward S Aarons had been an active writer since 1938, particularly using the pseudonym of Edward Ronns, he didn't create the character of Cajun CIA agent Sam Durell until 1955, but such was the popularity of Durell's 'assignments' that Aarons then chronicled roughly two a year for the rest of his life. The two assignments that launched the series in Italy were *Assignment – Burma Girl* from 1961 and *Assignment – Treason* from 1956, as *Operazione Birmania* and *Missione tradimento* respectively. In the latter story, Durrell is tasked with flushing out a traitor within the ranks of the CIA by himself masquerading as a traitor. When the impersonation becomes a little too convincing he is forced to go on the run. Further titles from just the next five years comprised volumes 20, 43, 58, 67, 81, 94, 104, 117, 123, 131, 137, 142 and 155.

Initially published monthly, the series switched to fortnightly with volume 16 in December 1962, with the schedule being dominated in the early years by the works of Jean Bruce. Of the first 100 volumes, 40 detailed the assignments of OSS 117 which, when added to series 1, makes 52 out of the first 112 volumes. Not unsurprisingly, this meant that France was the country most often represented in the early years, as Jean Bruce was far from the only French author who was translated. Le Fleuve Noir had been publishing in France since 1949, and one of their many ongoing imprints was the rather self-explanatory **Espionnage**. Some of the authors published by **Espionnage** and translated into **Segretissimo** in the early years included Alain Page, Richard Caron, MG Braun, Graham Livendert, Claude Rank and GJ Arnaud, while other French authors included Michel Carnal, Robert Julien Courtine (who was predominantly a food writer), Mike Cooper (pseudonym of Liliane M Gatineau), Jacques-Henri Juillet and Gilles-Maurice Dumoulin. The spies whose adventures were chronicled included Philippe Lar-

san, Serge Kovask – the Commander, Alex Glenne, Jasper Wood – who goes by the codename TTX 75 – and Jerry Jorsen, who has the codename JOSS 113. As far as I can gather, only Jean Bruce has ever been translated into English, and even then it was a mere fraction of his total output.

Volume 24 was the only time that a John D MacDonald novel was translated into a **Segretissimo**. His other works – including the Travis McGee novels – were predominantly released in Italy as part of the **Il Giallo Mondadori** series. Originally published in the US in 1954, *Area of Suspicion* was translated in April 1963 as *Nemico alle spalle*, and gradually evolves from a murder mystery (Gevan Dean investigating the death of his brother) into an industrial espionage tale set against the backdrop of the Cold War.

Robert Sheckley was a much-respected and prodigious author in the science fiction field, with his shorter work especially receiving great acclaim and adaptation, such as his 1953 short story 'The Seventh Victim' that

was turned into the 1965 vehicle for Ursula Andress, *La decima vittima* aka *The Tenth Victim*. Sheckley was also active in the espionage field and, although this particular aspect of his career is less well-known, the novels featuring CIA agent Stephen Dain have received acclaim from those knowledgeable of the genre. Only the first two books in the series of five appeared as a **Segretissimo** – *Calibre .50* for Volume 26 in May 1963 as *Calibro 50* and *Dead Run* for Volume 40 in November 1963 as the rather cumbersomely titled *Allarme! Chiamate Stephen Dain*. In the latter title, Dain is called in after a briefcase is stolen from agents on a London street by an innocuous thief named Carlos.

Volume 30 was *Operazione anti-catastrofe* by James Dark, originally published in 1962 as *Impact!* by Horwitz, the Australian publisher best known for Carter Brown. James Dark was a house name used primarily by JE MacDonnell for the 'Mark Hood' series of espionage novels, but *Impact!* and its sequel, *Havoc!*, were actually written by James Workman, a Scot who emigrated to Australia in the 1950s. Only *Impact!* was translated into a **Segretissimo**, detailing IMPACt operative Elliot Carr's investigation into the crash of the first moon rocket at an Australian Rocket Range. Incidentally, IMPACt stands for 'International and Metropolitan Police Air Control.'

The American writer Donald Hamilton, though he'd been writing professionally since the late 1940s, didn't debut the character of Matt Helm until 1960 in the novels *Death of a Citizen* and *The Wrecking Crew*, but Helm quickly became the American literary equivalent to the UK's James Bond. His adventures were chronicled by Hamilton over the course of the next 30 years in 27 novels, ending with *The Damagers* in 1993, though the four films starring Dean Martin, as is the way of Hollywood, bore little semblance to the source material. As originally envisioned by Hamilton, Helm was an assassin for OSS during the Second World War, with the codename 'Eric'. After living the comfortable life of a writer for fifteen years, he is brutally pulled back into the world of espionage to perform the task he is

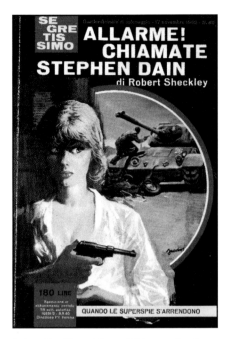

Robert Sheckley – Allarme! Chiamate Stephen Dain
(Dead Run – 1961)
Art - Carlo Jacono

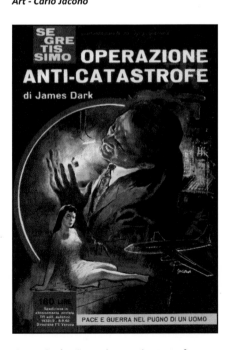

James Dark – Operazione anti-catastrofe
(Impact! – 1962)
Art - Carlo Jacono

most ably suited for – assassination. Volume 49 of **Segretissimo** was a translation of the 4th book in the series, *The Silencers*, published in March 1964 as *Doppio gioco*, quickly followed in June by Volume 56 *Nome di battiglia: Eric*, a translation of the 5th book, *Murderer's Row*. 1965 saw translations of the 6th and 7th books in Volumes 78 and 90, but it wasn't until September 1969 when the next translation appeared in Volume 304 – the 8th book *The Ravagers* as the verbosely titled *Riuscirà Matt Helm a salvare la figlia di tanta madre?*

Henry Patterson is better known, like Rene Raymond mentioned earlier, by one of his pseudonyms – in Patterson's case, Jack Higgins. Though Patterson had his first novel published in 1959, his major breakthrough novel was *The Eagle Has Landed* in 1975 under the Higgins pseudonym and from 1980 onwards he has only published under the name of Jack Higgins. Under the name of Martin Fallon, Patterson wrote a series of six novels in the 1960s starring Paul Chavasse, a British Agent working for the highly secretive agency called 'The Bureau'. The first book in the series, 1962's *The Testament of Caspar Schultz*, detailing the hunt for a document exposing the whereabouts of post-war Nazis, was translated into Volume 64 of **Segretissimo** in October 1964 as *Amburgo: si salvi chi può*. The second book, 1963's *Year of the Tiger* followed in June 1966 as Volume 136, *Paul Chavasse: operazione ricupero*, followed by books three and four in March 1967 and February 1968 respectively.

Doctor Jason Love was the 1964 creation of James Leasor, up until that time a journalist and writer of historical non-fiction such as *The One That Got Away*, but the success of Love's debut in *Passport to Oblivion* allowed Leasor to go full-time. Love, a country doctor who occasionally worked for MI6, eventually appeared in ten novels (and one film – *Where the Spies Are* starring David Niven) if

Donald Hamilton – Doppio gioco
(The Silencers – 1962)
Art - Carlo Jacono

Martin Fallon – Paul Chavasse: operazione ricupero
(Year of the Tiger – 1963)
Art - Carlo Jacono

SSS Sicario Servizio Speciale
(The Liquidator – 1964)
Art - Carlo Jacono

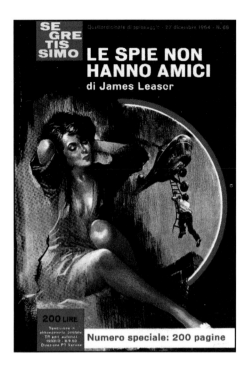

*James Leasor – Le Spie Non Hanno Amici
(Passport to Oblivion – 1964)
Art - Carlo Jacono*

you include *Host of Extras*, which crossed-over with another series, 'Aristo Autos'. *Passport to Oblivion*, where Love is persuaded to use a conference in Tehran as cover to find a missing British agent, was translated into **Segretissimo** Volume 69 and appeared as *Le spie non hanno amici* in December 1964. A sequel appeared early in 1966, *Passport to Peril*, and this was quickly translated in May's Volume 133 as *Dottor Love: operazione amore*, with the third book also being rapidly translated when it appeared the following year.

When Glidrose Productions, owners of the literary rights to James Bond, wanted to revive and update the character in the 1980s, they hired John Gardner, who eventually wrote sixteen novels – more than Fleming himself. The choice of Gardner was somewhat ironic given that his main literary claim

to fame was the creation of Boysie Oakes in the 1964 novel *The Liquidator*, a character that Gardner himself described as 'a piss-take' on the whole Bond phenomenon. The main conceit of the series was that Boysie Oakes was not the cold-hearted assassin his superiors thought him to be, but a fraud who was afraid of flying and who sub-contracted his assignments out to accomplished killers. *The Liquidator* was translated into volume 70 as *SSS Sicario Servizio Speciale* in January 1965, the same year that Rod Taylor and Trevor Howard starred in the, somewhat faithful, big screen adaptation. Gardner produced regular sequels throughout the 60s and early 70s, the series ending at eight books. However they weren't as regularly translated into volumes of **Segretissimo** – 1965's *Understrike* appeared as Volume 111's *Operazione: Playboy* in January 1966, 1966's *Amber Nine* wasn't translated at all, and 1967's *Madrigal* didn't appear until Volume 265's *Madrigale per il Liquidatore* in the very last week of December 1968. Gardner's James Bond novels were translated from 1991 onwards.

July 1965 saw **Segretissimo** switch to a weekly publishing schedule with the publication on the first of the month of Volume 83, *Fuochi d'artificio per OS 117*, another outing for Jean Bruce's OSS 117, this one being a translation of 1951's *L'arsenal sautera*.

End of part one. In issue 41, Rob Matthews continues his study of Segretissimo as the series continued into the 1970s.

Thanks to
- Randall Masteller at spyguysandgals.com for English language bibliographic information.
- Stefano at Libreria Eleste and Marco at FerifoxCartoon2015 for scans.
- Uraniamania.com and Archividiuruk.wordpress.com for Italian language bibliographic information.

JAMES DOIG explores the Australian paperbacks which mythologize Australia's equivalent of Times Square and Soho; the seedy area of Sydney known as Kings Cross.

KINGS CROSS PULP

Kings Cross is Sydney's version of London's Soho; since the early twentieth century it has had a place in the popular imagination as a bohemian sin-centre where strippers and prostitutes ply their trade alongside drug addicts, criminals, gamblers, occultists, actors and writers. Known as 'the Cross' or 'the glittering mile', it covers a small strip of the inner Sydney suburbs of Darlinghurst and Potts Point and is a byword for bohemianism, vice and a colourful, cosmopolitan lifestyle.

During the 1960s and '70s Kings Cross was an entertainment mecca with glittering nightclubs, strip clubs and seedy bars; it was constantly in the news, usually for all the wrong reasons. The average Australian was fascinated by Kings Cross and because of its notoriety a vigorous sub-genre of cheap paperback fiction (and non-fiction) emerged with the Cross featuring front and centre.

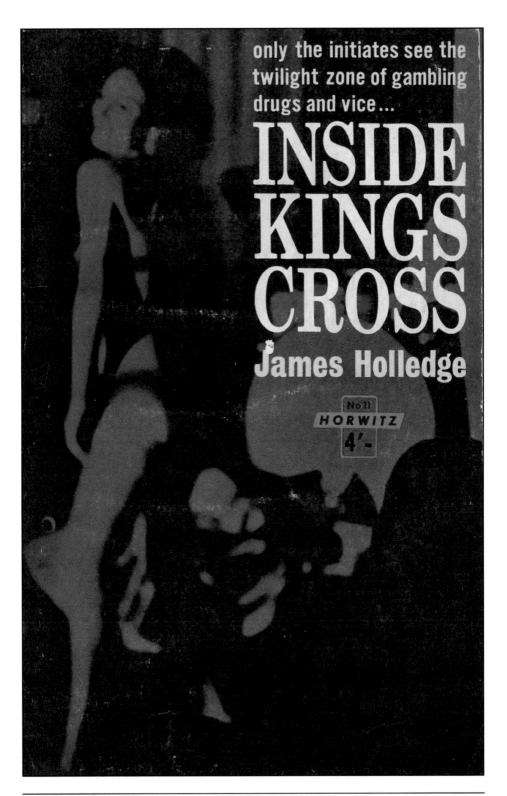

only the initiates see the twilight zone of gambling drugs and vice...

INSIDE KINGS CROSS

James Holledge

No.11
HORWITZ
4'-

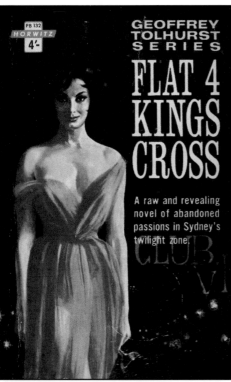

Most of these books were published by Horwitz, Australia's pre-eminent paperback publisher, and they usually had 'Kings Cross' splashed on the cover, either in the title or the salacious blurb ('The Kings Cross vice world taught her the other side of the profession').

In these books, the Cross is typically a lure to country folk looking to escape the tedium of the bush or respectable city-dwellers looking for excitement, or rebellious youth looking for a way out of the rat race. It's a place where you will lose your innocence but, if you're lucky enough to escape the vice trap, you will have learned something important about yourself.

An unusual feature of Kings Cross pulp is that much of it was written by women. Writers like Rena Cross, Marcia McEwan and Dianne Irwin remain obscure, but they published a group of novels about the Cross in the mid 1960s that are worth looking at in more detail.

Rena Cross (nee Dickman) was born in England in 1917 and came to Australia in 1950 where she worked as a cook on a Queensland cattle station. She later said she wrote her first short story there out of sheer boredom. Later Cross moved to South Australia where she began publishing short stories in magazines like *The Australian Woman's Weekly* as well as writing advertising copy and television scripts. She also had a passion for dogs, not only training them but also hosting a television show, 'Pets' Corner', on Adelaide's Channel 7.

By 1962 Cross had moved to Woollahra in Sydney's eastern suburbs where she joined the Horwitz stable of writers and began churning out novels. In a two-year period between 1962 and 1963 she published an astonishing nineteen novels, fifteen of them in 1963. A twentieth novel, under the house name John Duffy, was

published in 1965. Ten of the novels were medical romances written under the name Karen Miller; she also wrote for a couple of short-lived series under the names John Duffy (two of five novels in the series) and Rebecca Dee (two of four novels). Only one book was written under her own name, *Outback Heiress*, a semi-autobiographical novel about an English woman who becomes a station cook in outback Queensland.

Cross wrote at least two novels set in Kings Cross, *Flat 4 Kings Cross* (one of three novels she wrote under the name Geoffrey Tolhurst) and *Model School*, under the pseudonym Christine James.

Flat 4 Kings Cross was published in January 1963 and was popular enough to be reprinted at least twice, in 1965 and 1966. The book starts with the narrator, Carla, being locked up in prison for three years for prostitution. The rest of the book is her story about how she ended up there, having escaped a poor country upbringing and moving to the city aged fifteen. Already she seems to be morally tainted, having a reputation of being 'easy' or 'fast', and she has dark skin, inherited from her Afghan grandfather. After getting work in a café she comes under the influence of the *chic* Maria Grosnik, who runs an expensive gambling club with her husband. She offers Carla a job and Carla is soon installed in a penthouse at the top of the club, expensively coiffed, dressed and made up for the rich clientele. Disaster strikes when a patron is killed in a fight and Carla flees to the Gold Coast to avoid being called as a witness in the ensuing court case. She learns that the club has been closed and the Grosniks are going to be deported, but she returns to Sydney anyway, missing the excitement and high life. She finds it hard to get work, but is invited to take part in a 'private' film which turns out, much to her amusement, to be a black mass. There she

meets a former staffer of the Grosniks, Sammy, who tells her the club has reopened but under different management, and she gets work back at the club as a stripper. Carla falls for Johnny, the piano player, who is a heroin addict, but when he tries to inject her she knocks him unconscious with a vase and flees. She runs into Sammy again and he convinces her to set up on her own at Flat 4 Kings Cross:

'I could have worked every night of the week, if I had chosen. But I was still fussy over the men I met. I turned down more than I took home. I got the reputation for being very exclusive, and I heard that men even laid bets as to whether they could "make me" or not.'

Following another failed love affair, this time with a rich playboy, Garnet Wilde, who dumps her and sails off to Spain in his expensive boat, she is finally arrested for harbouring two girls who had absconded from reformatory school. The book ends with Carla receiving a letter from Wilde announcing he is returning to Australia to get Carla's case reopened and that they should consider themselves engaged, a ridiculous upbeat ending that is tacked on.

Model School was published in September 1963 and is a slight variation on the same theme. Eighteen-year old June Palmer lives in a country town, Berrawilla, 250 miles from Sydney, where she has always had a hankering to live. Finally her mum relents and gives her the money to move there where she finds a job in a casting agency, which suits June as she wants to be a top model or a TV star. She works for the manager's secretary, Margot Brown, who operates an escort business out of the agency, where girls are hired out to private parties. June is lonely and short of money and asks Margot if she could attend one of the parties; the experience isn't what she expected and she is saved

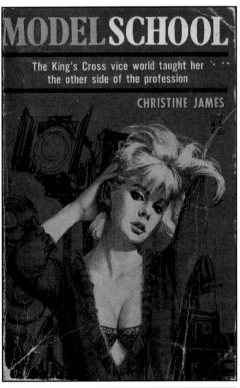

by the agency manager, Vic Dean, who subsequently takes her under his wing. June still has ambitions of becoming a model and joins the model school of the title, the Castleton School of Deportment and Drama, which turns out to be a scam and the long-suffering Vic has to rescue her once again. Meanwhile June catches up with two girls she met at the party, Bonnie and Nina, who reveal they are prostitutes earning the princely sum of £50 a week. Soon afterwards June leaves the casting agency under a cloud after arguing with Vic and runs into the manager of the scam model school who convinces her, with surprisingly few reservations from June, to act in a movie. Naturally, it turns out to be an adult movie and she just manages to escape by getting Nina to fill her part. Bonnie and Nina invite her to a party on a cruise ship, which turns nasty when Bonnie is glassed in the face and one of the men attempts to rape June. She jumps overboard, swims to shore, and is once again saved by Vic, who this time declares his love for her.

As these summaries suggest, *Flat 4 Kings Cross* and *Model School* have little to recommend them. They are made-to-order romance novels given a touch of spice by the Kings Cross setting, though there isn't enough grounding in the real Kings Cross to make the books in any sense realistic.

Rena Cross stopped writing for Horwitz in the mid 1960s and at some point she returned to England. From the early 1970s she produced a string of domestic self-help books starting with *The Manual of Home Freezing* in 1971 and continuing until about 1990 with titles like *The Complete Guide to Successful Parties* (1972), *Do Your Own Upholstery* (1975) and *Home Made Beers, Lagers and Stouts* (1982). She died in Worcestershire in 1997.

Marcia McEwan was a much more accomplished writer. Her career with Horwitz

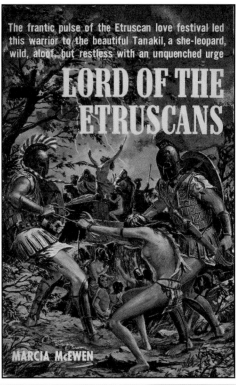

She lived with a wild push in a pad near the
Cross—living by their law

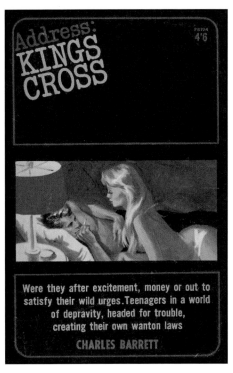

Were they after excitement, money or out to
satisfy their wild urges.Teenagers in a world
of depravity, headed for trouble,
creating their own wanton laws

CHARLES BARRETT

closely mirrored that of Cross: she wrote at least four Kings Cross pulps during a career that spanned 1964-1967 and nineteen novels. Her novels were quite varied and include historical romances like *Pharaoh, Roxana* and *Lord of the Etruscans*, all published in 1964, five spy novels written under the name James Scott, and youthsploitation novels such as *Beat Girl* (1965). Her Kings Cross novels focus on the vice and criminality of the Cross and the allure of money, sex and celebrity.

McEwan was born in 1929 and grew up in the Blue Mountain's apple-growing district of Little Hartley, not far from Lithgow, where her family were early pioneers. She had always wanted to be a writer and after finishing school became a journalist with the *Lithgow Mercury* before working for the publisher K G Murray in Sydney for whom she edited *True Romance*, *True Stories* and *Digest of Digests*.

In 1951 she left Australia for Europe, living for three years in Italy where she worked as a journalist for a British newsagency in Rome, writing scripts for an American production company on the lives of the great Italian composers, as well as working as a stunt double in a couple of Italian films. She appears to have spent some time in England as well as three months in Los Angeles learning how to write television scripts.

McEwan returned to Australia in October 1953 and the following year was working at Pagewood Studios in Sydney where she wrote scripts for the *Adventures of Long John Silver* television series as well as documentaries. She married a Dane, Wagner Osterberg-Olsen, and they settled in Lithgow where he managed the Lithgow Guest House Motel. In 1960 she won a television play contest, which was produced on Sydney's Channel 9.

McEwan began writing for Horwitz in 1964 and her first books were the trilogy of historical novels starting with *Pharaoh*, published in February 1964. Her fourth book was the racy *Address: Kings Cross*, published under the name Charles Barrett in September 1964.

The book is narrated by Claudine, a convent-educated rebel from Adelaide who has become a high-class call girl and arrested by the police in a sting. She tells the story of her fall from grace with an easy assurance that keeps you intrigued.

Unlike the Cross novels, Kings Cross is at the centre of the book, the author of Claudine's demise:

'Little more than a mile away from Sam's apartment was the Cross – Kings Cross, the vibrant, kaleidoscopic hub of Sydney's nightlife where people lived in a way I'd only dreamed about back in old-fogy Adelaide. At the Cross, things Happened. That's what I liked and needed, things happening all the time so that there were no empty hours to fill, no time to remember what a lousy deal life really was, anyway.'

She meets Greg Mitchell at a jazz club and within minutes tells her the history of Kings Cross:

'Even the type of life changes. It's always been nightlife, always hectic, but it has different angles. There was a gangster era in the late Twenties and the early depression years, the time of the razor gangs and dope and sly-grog peddlers. After the gangsters came the era of the Bohemians, the broke, struggling artists, actors and writers. The Cross was a place where they could live cheap and follow their unconventional ways of life without being bothered by the neighbours. Even when they became successful they stayed on here because it was a handy, easy-going place to live. And during the Fifties when a lot of continentals moved in, it

got to be cosmopolitan but quite respectable.'

Greg is a university dropout whose rich parents have bought him a run-down terrace in Paddington, and he shows her around the Cross, pointing out the sights and philosophising about the causes of juvenile delinquency and the hypocrisy of adults. In fact, much of the first half of the book is a sight-seeing tour of the Cross where we are introduced to the seamy underbelly of the district, in which violence, addiction and crime are rife.

Nevertheless, Claudine loves the excitement and thrill of life on the edge. When her father stops funding her profligate life style, she gets a job as a hostess in an exclusive restaurant and moves in with a beautiful stripper named Inge, who also works as a high-class call girl. Things take a turn for the worse when she loses her job and her rich boyfriend dumps her. She joins Inge working for Slim Kim, who runs the biggest call girl racket in the country. When her under-age friend, Billie, falls sick and can't take a job, Claudine switches places with her. However, it turns out the job was a set-up to have Chicago gangster Sam Penny locked up for having sex with a minor. Claudine is forced to prove her age and identity by contacting her outraged father, who sends her old flame Paul Constantine to bring her home. She tearfully agrees to marry him and to see a psychiatrist to sort out her behaviour, but the book ends with her planning to run away: 'The Cross is finished for me just now, but there are other cities. It would even be possible to go overseas, to see all the really lively, exciting places.'

The ambivalent ending is a nice touch; although Claudine comes across as a spoilt brat for most of the book, she does learn some humility from her experiences and we end up identifying with her.

Kings Cross Affair, published in July 1965, was written under the name Marsha Wayne and is a pedestrian crime thriller. Sarah Apsley is an English woman who arrives in Sydney to visit her friend, singer Marlene Dean, after being dumped by her boyfriend. Sarah is told Marlene has moved out the week before, but she turns up anyway and sees a couple of hoods bustling Marlene into a car. Sarah is helped by nondescript taxi driver, Ted Allen, and the two try to track Marlene down. After visiting Marlene's sister, who says her disappearance may have something to do with her boyfriend, Davide Carboni, Sarah is chloroformed and wakes up in a mortician's workshop, with a body next to her on a slab and coffins lined up against the wall. She's finally reunited with Marlene, who is being held in an attic room. Marlene tells Sarah they are dealing with an Australian branch of the mafia who run their operation out of Kings Cross; they had forced Davide to work for them, running drugs into Sydney. They manage to escape and are picked up by Ted and the handsome, urbane Matt Prentice from the Diplomatic Corps who had been trailing Sarah since she arrived in Australia. The word comes down from Matt's superiors that Sarah and Marlene are to be used as bait to capture the gang, which after the usual twists and turns is accomplished, the book ending with Sarah marrying the dashing Matt.

Vice Trap, Kings Cross, published in November 1966 under the name Jean-Paul Severn is also a crime thriller and is a stronger book. Warren Waters, who works for a bank, is found shot dead and the verdict is suicide. His brother Chuck, another innocent kid from the bush, wants to find out the truth and his investigation leads him to a vice empire running out of the Purple Garter Club in Kings Cross. McEwan takes the opportunity at every turn to show Chuck's shocked reaction to the excesses of Kings Cross, for example when he's served by a topless waitress at the Purple Garter:

'Chuck's answering grin froze on his face and an airlock in his windpipe threatened to choke him. He gulped. The girl was wearing a full skirt of some purple stuff. But if the outfit was supposed to include a blouse she had forgotten to put it on. She's even forgotten a bra...Chuck hid behind the menu, suddenly grateful for its size.'

Naturally, Chuck triumphs and exposes the blackmail business that drove his brother to suicide.

McEwan published a fourth Kings Cross pulp, *Night in Kings X*, under the similar but less exotic name, John Severn, in April 1965.

PB 285 60c

Vice trap, Kings Cross

The Purple Garter Club provided more than sexy striptease and topless go go. Young Chuck Waters gets mixed up in murder and mayhem at The Cross

Jean-Paul Severn

Joanne Joyce's *The Swingers*, published in 1967, is described on the first page as 'a brilliant first novel by a young Australian writer whose incisive style and inspiring insight bring to the reader a new understanding of the frightening dilemma facing today's delinquent youth.' Joanne Joyce was the pseudonym of Dianne Irwin, who wrote one other book for Horwitz, *It's All Right, Ma, I'm Only Sighing*, a Bob Dylan lyric, published in 1968. Nothing else is known about this author, but both of her books are brilliant youthsploitation novels and should be better known.

The Swingers is narrated by Jenny Adamson, a typically disaffected teenager, a New Zealander living in Sydney after being kicked out of home, who describes her aimless progression through a series of alcohol and drug fuelled parties:

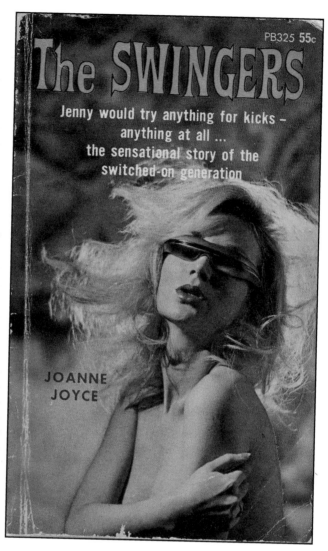

'The street throbbed with noise – a jangle of voices, the blaring of a record player as the Stones belted out *Paint it Black*. Someone sitting on the edge of the pavement was playing a mouth-organ, and the high notes were sweet over the top of the noisy hum of voices and music.'

While some of the kids are university students or art students at Tech, most are 'the drifters – beatniks who didn't work, but spent all their time at the pub and turned up at every party they heard about, existing most of the time on money they earned here and there which provided them with enough for cigarettes, flagons of rough red wine, and pills if they took them – and most of them did.' In fact, this pretty accurately describes Jenny herself, who is living on the last of the money her dad has given her. She gets stoned, pops pills, gets pissed on jars of wine, and has casual sex while high. She sees the raw side of life and is even offered a job as a prostitute in a massage parlour by a rich pimp.

The book is a fine read. There's a colourful cast of characters, like Johnny, who we meet briefly, rumoured to be writing a novel and who, when Jenny meets him, is 'eating yoghurt from a carton with a spoon and reading a lurid paperback, a Jack the Ripper saga of violence called *The Fiend of Golders Green*. Just what you'd expect an aspiring young novelist to be reading I thought, glancing at the very yellow-haired blonde who exposed two enormous breasts as she sprawled across the cover in a filmy negligee.'

At a party Jenny meets Mick, guitarist of an up-coming band called the Uglies, whose drummer had been deported back to England for dope possession. They hang out together and romance blooms at Poppy's, the Paddington nightclub where the band plays to heaving crowds. Jenny blows it by sleeping with someone else and then hitches to Melbourne with a friend, Mandy. There she goes on a pill-popping extravaganza that ends in a fatal car crash with Jenny the only survivor of the five who had piled into the mini. *The Swingers* is a fine first novel, a bleak, no-holds-barred portrayal of bored youth in 1960s Australia.

This is only a flavour of the many paperback pulps featuring Kings Cross published by Horwitz between 1963 and the early '70s, but they give a taste of the type of books the Horwitz editors thought would appeal to the reading public. The best of them show the colour and bustle of the Cross, show something of its character, and give an insight into its allure, the others are at least no worse than the mass of paperbacks published by Horwitz and its ilk.

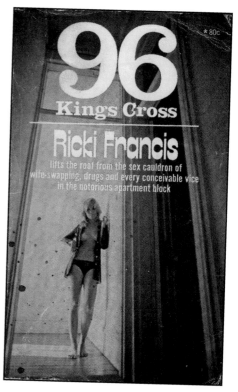

11405850R00037

Printed in Great Britain
by Amazon